P9-CAN-373

In YOUR OWN TRUE LOVE you will learn

How to build self-love through a succession of positive experiences.

How self-esteem begins, how it works, and how it shapes your life.

How to appreciate yourself and the people who care about you.

How to distinguish between self-love and self-centeredness; confidence and grandiosity.

How to take credit for the things you accomplish and accept praise for the person you are . . .
someone worthy of being loved!

"A remarkably candid book by a remarkably honest psychotherapist. Based on dozens of fascinating case histories, Dr. Robertiello has once again written a book in down-to-earth prose about what makes our mysterious psyches tick.

. . . I strongly recommend YOUR OWN TRUE LOVE as one sure way of enhancing your self-esteem."

—*Wilfred Quaytman, Ph.D.,*
Editor, Journal of Contemporary Psychology

YOUR OWN TRUE LOVE

*The new positive view of narcissism
The person you love the most should
be ... you*

Richard C. Robertiello, M.D.

BALLANTINE BOOKS • NEW YORK

Lines in Chapter III from *The Metamorphoses of Ovid—An English Version* by A. E. Watts. Copyright © 1954 by The Regents of the University of California: Reprinted by permission of the University of California Press.

Copyright © 1978 by Richard C. Robertiello, M.D.

All rights reserved. No part of this book may be reproduced in any form or by any means without the prior written permission of the Publisher, excepting brief quotes used in connection with reviews written specifically for inclusion in a magazine or newspaper. For information write to Richard Marek Publishers, Inc., 200 Madison Avenue, New York, N.Y. 10016. Published in the United States by Ballantine Books, a division of Random House, Inc., New York, and simultaneously in Canada by Random House of Canada, Limited, Toronto, Canada.

Library of Congress Catalog Card Number: 78-6051

ISBN 0-345-28297-3

This edition published by arrangement with Richard Marek Publishers

Manufactured in the United States of America

First Ballantine Books Edition: October 1979

To Dr. Heinz Kohut, the world's greatest living psychoanalyst, whose pioneer work on narcissism inspired this book.

I would like to acknowledge my appreciation to my wife, Robbi, several of my patients and colleagues, my editor, Ms. Joyce Engelson, and my agent, Mr. Don Congdon, for their very meaningful suggestions and their constant support and encouragement in writing this book. And I would especially like to single out Ms. Nancy Friday, Mr. Lawrence Hauser, Mr. Bill Manville and Dr. Selma Mindes for their thoughtful recommendations.

CONTENTS

CHAPTER 1

Self-esteem, Self-effacement, Self-centeredness, and Grandiosity

Who is "your own true love?" Who is the person you love the most? It may be something of a surprise to you, but unless the anwer is "you," you are in trouble. When Harry Stack Sullivan, a famous American psychoanalyst, was asked to define love, he gave what I consider to be one of the best definitions. He said that you love someone when you are concerned about his or her security and satisfaction almost as much as you are about your own. That implies, of course, that you should never be as concerned about anyone else over any extended period of time as much as you are concerned about yourself.

Yet society in general, and even psychoanalysts in particular, have been very much split and very much confused about the issue of self-love. There seem to be two kinds of self-love—a good kind and a bad kind. If you have a healthy regard for yourself and an appreciation of your strengths, a high *self-esteem*, obviously that has to be good. Having confidence, as it is also called by some, gives you the strength to dare to attempt some adventures that may be fun or profitable and that you would be timid about otherwise. Having a good opinion of yourself is also important to buttress you against failures and misfortunes, those you may bring about yourself or those that occur by chance without your direct responsibility for them—like losing a job or a loved one or contracting a serious illness.

But there is a bad kind of self-love, too. What about the person who is constantly paying attention to himself or herself, or who is compulsively trying to get the attention of others? These people's self-love does not seem to grow out of confidence, but rather the opposite. The person who looks in the mirror continuously or brags about his latest conquest or is preoccupied with his last illness or operation does not seem to be acting out of a sense of security, but rather out of a feeling of *not* counting enough. He does not have a high self-esteem; instead, he is *self-centered*.

So, first of all, we must distinguish between a healthy good feeling of concern and appreciation about oneself and a compulsive attention-paying to or attention-seeking for oneself. Also, we must distinguish objectively between who we *really* are and what we *feel* we are. Some rather unattractive people *feel* attractive and communicate this, often so well that we are actually caught up in their own positive view of themselves. Some very attractive people clearly feel and act as if they are not—and this feeling is also often communicated by them to the people around them. So one of our first differentiations must be between our objective selves and our subjective feeling about ourselves—our *self-image*.

To complicate matters even further, we must try to fit into our scheme of things those people who have an absolutely irrationally inflated view of themselves, who are carried away with their own importance beyond the limits of reality. Psychoanalysts and others call these people *grandiose*, and the condition they suffer from *grandiosity* or illusions of grandeur. A good contemporary example of such a grandiose person is Idi Amin, the President of Uganda. People who are grandiose, like Idi Amin, often have a simple child-like quality, but frequently, in their very naïveté, they can be both destructive and self-destructive.

We have to try to see what the relationship is among

grandiosity, self-effacement or low self-esteem, self-centeredness, and healthy self-esteem. To put it in a nutshell, we all go through a period in our infancy when it is normal to be very grandiose. As babies we feel as if the whole world revolves around us. We cry and mother brings us our milk. Sometimes she knows we are hungry even before we are conscious of it. As babies we really seem to be at the center of the universe. We are admired by people as if we were the world's greatest creation. Our needs to be fed, changed, warmed are met almost before we express them, or very shortly thereafter. Being grandiose at that age level is or should be a normal state of affairs. And if, in fact, our grandiosity is relatively well-satisfied at that age-appropriate time, we are apt to have just about our fill of it. Along with this, we are likely to develop a pretty good feeling about ourselves, since we get such a positive response from our environment without really having to do very much but lie there in order to get it.

But if we don't get enough adoration and if our need to feel grandiose isn't well enough fed at that point, then we tend to continue to harbor a need to have this grandiosity affirmed later in our lives. Unsatisfied, the need may linger. And it is one thing to expect others to adore you and respond to your unspoken needs when you are an infant, and quite another to expect this to happen when you are an older child or an adult. In fact, most of us just don't get quite enough satisfaction for these needs in our infancies. We carry around with us hope in the form of fantasies of being the greatest, most special person in the whole world, just as we seemed to be when very young. These illusions of grandeur in adulthood seem so inappropriate, even insane to us, that most of us repress them completely. As a matter of fact, most of us are so afraid that our grandiosity, if fed, might get out of hand, we tend to suppress even normal good feelings about ourselves, or at least are afraid to accept well-justified and deserved praise. You know how embarrassed you or some of

your friends sometimes are when you are complimented. One of the main reasons for this is our fear of becoming just like a swell-headed, omnipotent, grandiose
little baby. We can't even allow ourselves to receive ordinary praise that is appropriate and merited. So our
very *fear* of grandiosity can lead to *self-effacement*, a
lowered self-esteem, a lack of appreciation of what we
have, and an inability to absorb the good things that
come our way. And this, of course, can lead to a
chronic low self-esteem. Then we are constantly at the
mercy of any bad, unlucky, perplexing things that may
happen to us because these will not be buffered by the
shock absorbers of a healthy self-esteem.

If we lose our job, if we are reprimanded by our
boss, if we are rejected by our loved one, if we fail in
sex, if we get sick, if we lose a game, if our friend does
not call or return our dinner invitation, if our book
does not become a best-seller, we take it very hard. We
flagellate ourselves and feel that we are total failures.
For some of us, a slight or a humiliation can so lower
our self-esteem that we even contemplate suicide. Not
long ago, a diplomat was criticized about a minor question in his expense account for which he might not
even have been guilty. Feeling totally humiliated, apparently unable to call upon his basic self-esteem, he
jumped out of a window.

We really do need a high, stable level of self-love to
cushion life's misfortunes and those mistakes that even
the best of us will sometimes make. Even Joe DiMaggio did drop a fly ball once in a while. We need to give
ourselves *the right to be wrong.* This is certainly as important as the inalienable rights provided by our constitution. If we have a healthy level of self-love, we will
be compassionate to ourselves and forgiving of our
mistakes. If we do not, we may be merciless and puni-
tive to ourselves. Conversely, if we have a fear of loving ourselves too much (a fear of our grandiosity), we
may not be able to appreciate fully our good qualities,
our good fortune, or our successes, or to accept admiring responses to us of others.

Some of us who don't like ourselves enough—for reasons we will discuss later—just go through life hiding, basically accepting our inferiority. We have a much lower self-image than we should have objectively. We are shy or timid about putting ourselves forward or choosing the limelight. So we go through life feeling bad about ourselves and missing out on many opportunities, many challenges we would have attempted with a better image of ourselves. We avoid competing. We are humble, modest, *self-effacing*.

On the other hand, some people with this apparently same low self-esteem, this poor sense of themselves, constantly and even compulsively try to repair it. They are the people who are absorbed in themselves and trying hard to get others to join them in this absorption. Most of us call them "narcissistic," in the negative sense of the word. They are always looking in the mirror, worried about a pimple, bragging about their accomplishments, talking incessantly, or otherwise "coming on." They do not have high self-esteem; what they are is *self-centered*. They can be amusing and attractive for a while, but over the long haul they are usually annoying because of their unending demand to have their needs met and their indifference to our needs. No amount of attention is enough for them. So we define the first type of person as *self-effacing* and we define this type as *self-centered*. We must remember, though, that these self-centered people really have a *low* self-image and are compulsively trying to repair it.

There is another, rarer, type. This is the person who is *grandiose*, who really has illusions of grandeur. His illusions aren't attempts to repair a low self-image. He really has a very inflated view of his own importance. Often this view has been sustained and reflected by his past environment or his current one. He has had in the past or in the present deficient outside controls over his grandiosity and gets carried away with himself, often to the eventual detriment of the people around him and eventually to himself. Not too many people fit into this uncommon category—some entertainers, war heroes, sports idols, and political leaders—but it is an important group for us to understand. People like this can have a tremendous effect on the world—especially if they become dictators! And people like this can give us an idea of why we are so afraid of our own grandiosity: the possibility of its getting out of hand. We are afraid of being thought of as swell-headed. We fear being humiliated if we fail to live up to the image, and we fear being destructive and/or self-destructive if we do.

The relationship of grandiosity to self-esteem, self-effacement, and self-centeredness is complicated, as you see. If you haven't grasped it at this moment, don't despair. Much of this book is concerned with explaining it and giving examples of it. Also I will try to explore the roots in our own individual development of all of these issues.

More important in some ways than all these explanations, you will want to know, "Is there anything I can do about my image of me, my self-esteem? Is it fixed in childhood? Or is it fixed by the time I have grown up? Is there anything I can do *now* to change the way I feel about myself? Can reading this book really help?" The answer to those questions is, happily, that our image of ourselves can change even very late in our lives. Our understanding of the process that keeps our self-image and self-esteem so low, and may or may not trigger useless, distasteful efforts at repair, can be modified by an educational approach, such as reading this book. Though there may not be much help for the person with true illusions of grandeur, he would probably not be reading this book anyway. And once aware of what such people are like, we can detect them more quickly and we can avoid them.

All this seems to me a rather tall order of promises; I am afraid you may think that I must be rather grandiose myself to make them. In fact, I would be grandiose if you took the promises too literally, if you thought I could transform you immediately from self-effacing and shy to self-confident and outgoing just by recommending that you read my book. I don't think I *can* promise that, but I do feel confident that understanding these issues of self-esteem can truly help you to deal with them. Dr. Heinz Kohut's books, *The Analysis of the Self* and *The Restoration of the Self,* certainly had a profound effect on me. Reading them stimulated the beginning of needed changes in my own self-image. Indeed, I would recommend Dr. Kohut's books to all of you, except that they are very technical and difficult for even a professional to understand. So this book, *Your Own True Love,* was stimulated by my desire to communicate Dr. Kohut's ideas in a manner that everyone can understand. In addition, it contains many examples from my clinical and personal experience, and hopefully some helpful and clarifying ideas of my own.

Recently there has been a good deal of concern among many writers and commentators on the social climate in America over the intense preoccupation with "self" that seems to have surfaced in our society. It appears to me that this trend is unmistakable. Many sociologists, social historians, psychologists, and psychoanalysts have pointed out correctly—both in the individual and in society—a trend that involves a focus on the self, leading away from relationships to other individuals, family, and community. They have correctly noted an increasing interest in psychic survival and a shrinking interest in personal relationships, social change and politics. When this condition reaches an extreme, we have a totally alienated person—an individual who is interested only in his own image and his own aggrandisement, whose contacts are based only on momentary self-gratification and self-enhancement. These individuals are, in fact, often rewarded by our society in terms of business, political, financial, and even social and sexual success. However, they suffer from an inner sense of isolation, loneliness, and a constant need to accumulate more and more power and admiration. Very likely the reason for this change in ourselves and our society is related to the change from the tightly knit, emotionally close nuclear and extended family to our present families of fewer children, diminishing contact between parents and children, and more frequent geographical and emotional separation between the individual and his nuclear and/or extended family. The erosion of close ties leads to a strong new need to focus on individual survival, to depend less on contacts with other individuals, groups, or systems, and to count on oneself alone. While these are clearly negative results of a certain kind of focus on the self, at the same time this focus may also produce more positive results in terms of self-reliance, self-fulfillment and self-realization. It may produce more individual creativity and artistic and scientific originality. Understanding the issues in this book may give the reader a conceptual base on which these individual and larger social changes can be placed.

CHAPTER 2

Questionnaire:
How Much Do You Really
Love Yourself?

Now that I have given you a brief explanation of self-esteem, I'd like to involve you in the subject in a more personal way by giving you a test. This is designed to help you focus in a very specific way on some of the issues I have raised in the introduction, and to give you a useful appraisal of your own level of healthy self-esteem. Hopefully it will also begin to clarify for you whether you are a self-effacing person—too modest and shy, a person self-centered in the negative sense of the word, or a person with a healthy balance of self-love. In any event, even though you already know more than a little about what constitutes a plus and a minus, try to be as honest as you can be in answering the fifty questions below with either "yes" or "no."

1. I generally put my best foot forward.
2. I pay attention to my appearance and try to look attractive.
3. I feel good about how I look. I like my face and my body.
4. I go into a room without comparing my physical attractiveness with others there.
5. I feel I have good taste.
6. I feel I am quite intelligent.

7. When I'm in a group or class, I feel as if I can hold my own with my peers.

8. I feel I do a good job at my work.

9. I feel I have my share of assets in other areas.

10. I like to receive praise and compliments. They don't make me feel foolish and nervous.

11. I can give compliments easily and generously.

12. I don't get nervous when I'm having guests at my home.

13. I don't get nervous when I have to address a group.

14. I don't feel nervous when the boss calls me in. I expect to get a raise rather than to be fired.

15. I feel as if I am a good parent or sibling or child.

16. When someone appreciates me, I don't try to deny the good things they're saying about me.

17. I think I am basically a good, kind person and seldom feel guilty and unworthy.

18. I can accept constructive criticism graciously.

19. I am not easily hurt or thin-skinned.

20. I rarely blush.

21. I rarely feel embarrassed.

22. I don't get hurt or feel humiliated if I am slighted.

23. I don't get furious or depressed if I am not waited on promptly.

24. I do the best I can to get the attention and admiration I think I deserve.

25. I think as much of myself as my closest friends think of me.

26. When I do something well, I give myself credit for it, rather than thinking I was lucky.

27. I do not get upset about blemishes on my skin.

28. When meeting people, I think about whether others will be good enough for me, rather than whether I will be good enough for them.

29. I expect to be accepted by most people I meet.

30. I have fantasies of being great or famous.

31. I am generally neither shy nor ill-at-ease with new people.

32. When I do (or did) go out on dates, I expect (or

expected) to be thought of as attractive and desirable.

33. I am aware of my sexuality and expect a response to it.
34. I take good care of my body.
35. When outside events beyond my control go wrong, I don't run myself down.
36. I am not the first person I blame.
37. I am not overly humble, modest, or self-effacing.
38. I enjoy showing off my good points and getting positive attention for them. I like to be in the limelight.
39. I don't feel uncomfortable if I am placed appropriately in a position of authority.
40. If I am good at something, I feel comfortable acknowledging it.
41. I like people on the basis of their personality, rather than their credentials.
42. I do not pick my friends on the basis of status.
43. I think I have made wise choices in intimate friends.
44. I generally feel my friends like and value me.
45. I do not feel embarrassed when the person I accompany makes a faux pas.
46. I feel proud about the person I have picked as my mate.
47. I am *not* preoccupied about my health.
48. I don't worry about getting old.
49. I'm not concerned about wrinkles or balding or other signs of aging.
50. I feel good about my sexual life.

Well, how did you come out? If you had more than twenty-five no's, you may well have some problem about your self-esteem. In that case, this book may help you. If you had fewer than twenty-five no's, you're in better shape about your feelings about you than many people. This book may not be as crucial for you personally, except that, in helping to explain about others, it will facilitate your relationships with them. Hopefully it may be interesting to you, too!

Remember that your score is not fixed for life. It is important only that you have an idea of where you stand on these emotional issues as you begin to read this book. If you and I are lucky, perhaps you can take the test over again a while after you have finished the book to see if there has been any change. I recommend a time lapse of a year; the book is not really expected to change you immediately. Hopefully, however, it will start a process of germination of a good many ideas which will gradually and subtly begin to come to fruition, given time.

Also, I am a big believer in success breeding success. Putting some of the ideas in this book into practice may be difficult in the beginning. But, if you persist, some success after a first try will make it easier the second time around. And so on. Keep a record of your initial score, and then try the same test exactly a year from now. I'd really like to know if your score changes. It will help me to formulate ideas for myself and my colleagues. So whether you do better or worse or stay exactly the same, please write and let me know. And feel free to include any comments—positive or negative—that you may want to make about the book, along with changes up or down in your test score. Your letters will help me to evaluate the impact of the book, and share this information with other professionals and, ultimately, with you.

Please send the results to me at: 49 East 78th Street
New York, N.Y. 10021

CHAPTER 3

The Greatest Taboo of All—Self-love

Our society comes down pretty hard on many things—sex, dirt, gluttony, theft, violence. But often, in our culture, the one aspect of ourselves we feel most individual shame about is self-love. Is there anything quite so humiliating, for example, as having the courage to praise yourself and then hearing someone laugh at you? That is mortifying to most of us. And is there any more insulting comment than that someone is vain, egotistical, in love with himself? In our society, narcissism—the fancier psychoanalytic word for self-love—is a dirty word. The Bible warns us—"Vanity, vanity, all is vanity." A person would rather be called anything but vain. Americans especially often seem to put a great premium on humility. Clever politicians almost always try to appear humble. Our President, Jimmy Carter, presents himself as a man of the people, asking for their help, and God's, to find the way. Generally, in this country, we have a distaste for the braggart and admiration for the quiet, self-effacing, modest person. The typical American movie hero used to be the strong, silent type like Gary Cooper or Jimmy Stewart.

Why is self-love or self-praise so unpleasant to us? Sometimes, in group therapy, I set up an exercise in which I ask each member to pretend that he has died the day before, and that he is a good friend delivering the eulogy at the funeral. It is amazing how difficult it is for anyone to say anything good about himself. Most people find it hard to get out even one or two phrases. And often they follow these with denials or detractions. I had one patient who literally broke into tears and ran out of the room when his turn came. The very contemplation of saying something good about himself panicked him.

The word "narcissism" comes from the myth of the Greek god Narcissus, who was so beautiful that he looked at his reflection in a lake until he died.

The ancient Greeks had the idea that the punishment for self-love was death. They also felt that too much love of self precluded love of anyone else. It would be helpful for us to get to the root of the word by quoting some passages from Ovid's *Metamorphosis III* about Narcissus. (From *The Metamorphosis of Ovid—An English Version by A.E. Watts, University of California Press, Berkeley, 1954.*)

Ovid, *Metamorphosis*, III

For when Narcissus, sixteen years gone by,
As boy or man could take a lover's eye,
His tender bloom concealed such hard disdain
That man and maiden wooed alike in vain.
Once, as he spread his nets and drove the deer,
Echo, the nymph of answering voice stood near ...
And now when she sees Narcissus, as he roves
O'er hill and dale, and as she sees, she loves;
And dogs his steps, unseen; and as she goes
Nearer the source, her fire the fiercer glows.
With torches dipped in sulphur 'tis the same,
Which near the fire are quick to catch the flame.
How oft she wished to whisper, drawing near,
Soft prayers and tender speeches in his ear,
But lacked an opening, by her nature driven
To wait his words, and give back what was given.

By chance the youth, who missed his comrades, cried:
"Is any here?" and "Here," the nymph replied.
Amazed, he looked all round him, but in vain;
And calling: "Come," himself was called again.
He looked behind, and called, as none was nigh,
"Why shun me?" and received the same reply.
Then, still deluded by the mocking sound,
He cried: "Here let us meet." and stood his ground;
And willing Echo (never sound more sweet
Would claim her answer) answered: "Let us meet."
To back her words, she left the wood, and went
To clasp his neck: such hope his speech had lent.
He fled, and fleeing shouted: "Let me be:
Death be my portion ere I yield to thee."
And here, by heat and hunting tired, one day,
Beside the pleasant pool Narcissus lay;
And bending over, quenched his thirst, to find
Within his heart a thirst of different kind;
Loving a phantom, it was his to feel
Delusive hope, and think a vision real;
Self-hypnotized, he could not look away,
But like a statue, fixed in pose he lay
Face downward on the margin of the mere,
Seeing his eyes, twin stars, reflected clear;
His beardless cheek, his ivory neck, his hair,
As that of Bacchus or Apollo fair;
And features and complexion, fair to view,
Where blushing rose and lily blend their hue.
  Strange love, when he who kindles feels the flame,
And gives the praise his own perfections claim;
Himself admiring, by himself admired,
Lover and loved, desiring and desired.
Not knowing what he sees, he sees and burns;
The cheating vision spurs his love, and spurns;
From lips, from eyes, the floating mockery flees;
He cannot clasp, nor kiss, the self he sees.
In vain, fond boy, you clutch a fleeting ghost;
That which you love—but turn aside, 'tis lost;
That which you seek, the form at which you stare,
Is mere reflection, neither here nor there;

Nought in itself, it stays but while you stay,
And could you go, with you would go away.
  No thought of food could tear him from the place,
No thought of sleep; he watched the feigning face
With never sated eyes; and so he lay
While through his eyes his life-force ebbed away.
With arms outstretched, half-rising from the ground,
He thus addressed the woods that clustered round:
"O woodlands wise, the lover's friendly screen,
Has e'er a lover so tormented been:
Can you, whose lives through generations go,
Remember one by loving brought so low;
So fair a form I see: deceit unkind,
That what I see and love I cannot find.
Less grief it were, did oceans separate,
Or road, or range, or city's close-barred gate.
A little water parts us, and a space
Of next to nothing hinders our embrace.
My arms, which almost touch, he strives to greet;
With face upturned he strains my lips to meet.
But ah, you cheat me, boy beyond compare,
I know not why, and flee, I know not where.
Come forth, be known: you have no cause to fly
My age and looks: the love of nymphs am I.
Some friendly promise in your face I view;
You stretch your arms, when I stretch mine to you;
Smile when I smile, and answer tears with tears,
And send the message back my gesture bears;
And since your sweet lips move, I think they say
Words that, before they reach me, die away.
  "Ah, cheat no more: we two, I see, are one:
I love myself, and scorch in my own sun.
Must I be sued, or sue: What boon procure:
My loved one's mine: possession makes me poor.
Oh, could I leave this body, and remove
(Was e'er such lover's prayer?) from what I love!
My sorrow saps my strength; no portion long
Of life is left; I perish, though so young.
And death, which ends my grief, is light to me:

I would my loved one's life could longer be;
But we, so coupled, two in one must die."
Then to the lure again he turns his eye,
And weeps, distraught, and ruffles with his tears
The surface, and his semblance disappears.
When this he saw, "O cruel," was his cry;
"Oh stay, from him that loves you do not fly.
Oh be it given, if not to touch, to see,
And feed my madness and my misery."
    With hands as cold as marble, blow on blow.
Beneath the blows it changed from white to red,
Like apples which the ripening tints o'erspread,
Or grapes that fleck the bunch with purplish hue;
This sight the pool, resettling, mirrored true.
This broke his heart: like wax in gentle heat,
Or morning frosts the first mild sunbeams meet,
Dissolved to dew, he wasted with desire,
Chafed inwardly by slow and secret fire.
Now from his cheek the rose and lily fly,
His pride and power, and all that pleased the eye.
Gone was the form that Echo loved in vain;
And she, though fretted still by rage and pain,
Sorrowed to see him thus, and as he cried
"Alas!" each time her word to his replied.
At times he beat his breast, and as he beat,
She answered every sound in counterfeit,
"Boy, loved in vain"——he spoke his latest word
Watching the pool with gaze that never stirred;
And as "In vain," reechoed from the dell,
"Farewell," he cried, and Echo cried: "Farewell."
    Now sank his weary head, and death shut fast
Eyes that admired their owner to the last;
Who now a ghost upon the Stygian shore
Gazed at his own reflection as before
His sisters mourn, the nymphs of stream and spring,
And sorrow's tribute, severed locks, they bring;
His cousins too, the woodland nymphs, lament;
And answering Echo joins in sad consent.
But now, when pyre and catafalque and flare

Wait the last rite, they find no body there:
No body, but a flower, their eyes behold,
White rays in circle round a heart of gold.

In this poem, Narcissus, an exceptionally beautiful sixteen-year-old boy, hard and disdainful, scorned the love of all others. The nymph, Echo, fell in love with him. She approached him but he shunned her. Then one day he lay down tired beside a pool. Seeing his reflection, he was so smitten by his own beauty that he fell in love with it. Not knowing it was only a reflection of himself, he tried to clasp it or kiss it, but naturally was unable to do so. Frustrated and tormented by not being able to possess what he really loved, he grieved and grieved. Unable to eat or sleep, he gradually withered away and died. When mourners came for him, even his body had disappeared. All that was left of him was a flower next to the pool.

It does not take deep analysis to see that, in this poem, Narcissus was clearly the victim of the "bad" kind of self-love. He was self-centered, rather than possessed of a high self-esteem. He was so obsessed with his image that he could not become involved with Echo or with anyone else. People who are self-centered have difficulty in really caring about or relating to others. A cartoon in the *New Yorker* showed Narcissus sitting by his pool. Echo, sitting next to him, gazes into his eyes and says, "Is there someone else?"

But the poem, besides making the point that Narcissus was unable to become involved with anyone else, also yields other ideas. The preoccupation with himself was frustrating and became an obsession with Narcissus. He could never really satisfy his need for more and still more admiration of himself. This is also a characteristic of self-centeredness. People who are self-centered can never get enough adulation, and perhaps they, too, tend to wither away and die, in an emotional sense. Like Narcissus, they can never satisfy their own need for more and more admiration and, since they cannot really ever accept any loving attention from others (even when they do get it, as Narcissus did from Echo), their emotional life becomes impoverished. They, like Narcissus, almost turn into addicts, caught up in the process of "feeding their habit," so that the rest of life and all other people become meaningless to them, they sometimes literally as well as figuratively wither away and die.

The idea that if you love yourself too much you can't have enough love left for anyone else was espoused, even by psychoanalysts, for years. However, some analysts have changed their ideas about this recently and think that self-love is healthy, but there remains, in many psychoanalytic circles, a strong tendency to feel that the quality of loving one's self is in direct opposition to the ability to love others—and is, therefore, a manifestation of illness. Personally, I think this is just an example of psychoanalysis itself being caught up in negative attitudes about self-love, along with the rest of our culture. And, of course, if one makes the distinction between high self-esteem and self-centeredness (people with high self-esteem can love others; people who are self-centered cannot), this apparent contradiction is resolved.

Actually, there are two different views in the psychoanalytic community. One view (supported especially by a New York analyst, Dr. Otto Kernberg), sees self-love as a haven for those who do not have the capacity to love others. He considers it, as does the general culture, a deviation from normal development, rather than a part of it. The other view is advocated by Dr. Heinz Kohut of Chicago, who feels that self-love and its growth are part of a natural developmental process. Even though I am from New York, I definitely share the view of Dr. Kohut on this issue; I feel that self-love is a healthy element of our development. And I think problems growing out of the issues of self-love relate to lack of enough admiration in childhood. As a result, certain mechanisms may develop that prevent an individual from *ever* taking in enough (or *any*) love and admiration in later life. I try to help people to attract, and then to absorb, more admiration, rather than to view self-love as a way of avoiding the love of others. The old truism that you can't really love anyone else if you don't love yourself makes a lot of sense to me. What has confused people, I believe, is the inability to make the distinction between *self-esteem* and *self-centeredness*. This confusion has seeped into analytic thinking, as well as into the popular view, and has created a great many problems besides the semantic ones.

Our society puts a double bind on us over self-love and admiration. By a double bind I mean we get two contradictory and mutually exclusive messages. For instance, there are many paintings about the Adoration of the Christ child by the Magi, and, indeed we actually seem to worship very young infants and children. But when they get a little older—starting even during the second year of life—we ridicule them if they do things to call attention to themselves. Suddenly, to seek the admiration we gave them so freely when they were infants becomes a shameful act for which we heap humiliation on them. The confusion is very difficult for a child to endure. And, of course, this condemnation of praise- and adulation-seeking continues and is constantly reinforced into their adult lives. They are called vain and egotistical if they speak or behave in a way that is calculated to encourage praise.

Why does society's attitude change so rapidly and so drastically between the period of infancy-to-early-childhood and the older years? Why are we so turned off by someone commending himself or trying to elicit praise by appearance or behavior? These are some of the questions we must try to answer in this book.

In terms of how *you* feel about *yourself*, as I have said, I am very hopeful of having a positive impact because I was able to change much of my handling of my own feelings about myself after reading Dr. Kohut's technical books. I would like to convey to you some of the spirit of his work. My aim is to help you to handle your own feelings about yourself in a way that en-

hances you and makes you feel good about yourself—
to praise yourself appropriately, seek admiration in
suitable ways, and be able to receive compliments that
are sincerely meant and deserved. If reading this book
can effect all this—and I sincerely believe it can
help—then my own task will be accomplished. I will
be able to congratulate myself and solicit, and take in,
whatever praise you, the reader, have for me. And
hopefully, by the time you finish this book, *you* will be
able to congratulate yourself for having had the good
sense to buy and read it without feeling ashamed of
being vain or egotistical. I will have been able to con-
vince you that self-love is *not* necessarily a dirty word,
and you will have been able to transcend the greatest
taboo of them all.

The semantic difference between self-esteem and
self-centeredness has never been very clear to anyone.
All of us, professional or not, have mixed up these two
qualities, often using the same words to describe both
of them. Words are very powerful. A psychoanalyst,
after all, uses little but words. They can have a tremendous influence on how we feel about ourselves, what
we reward and what we punish, what ideas we pass on
to our children, even on what we believe to be real.
The confusion over the term "self-love" has, I think,
caused a tremendous amount of difficulty for all of us.
For this reason, if for no other, I feel strongly that a
direct educational approach, such as reading this book,
can have a very powerful impact on the way you will
be able to regard yourself.

CHAPTER 4

Self-love is Not a Dirty Word

Rather than being a dirty word, self-love is, in the best sense—that is, self-esteem—an honorable word, describing an extremely necessary and important feature of personality. If we don't have a substantial reserve of self-esteem "in the bank," we are always in trouble. Even the mildest criticism can be neither buffered nor assimilated as a constructive suggestion; we have no reserve to combat it. We may feel either totally destroyed or become ultradefensive, putting up such a fight against the criticism (because we are *so* vulnerable to letting it in) that people will view us as stubborn, difficult, even obnoxious. After knowing us for a while, they will be so afraid to say anything that might hurt us, they will tend to avoid us literally, or else avoid communicating any honest feelings to us—in effect, avoiding true emotional contact with us. As a result, we feel lonely, alienated, and shunned. This, of course, will tend to lower our self-esteem even more, so we become even more defensive. The snowball effect leaves us more and more isolated. We can see, therefore, that a reasonable degree of self-esteem is really *essential* to our well-being.

But what is a reasonable degree? What about the braggart, preening himself, continually seeking attention? If having a reasonable degree of self-love means being like him, then who would want it? The question really is: how does a person who focuses on himself completely rate himself in terms of self-love? What is the extent of the braggart's self-esteem, the show off's self-image? Well, even though it *seems* as if he has too much self-love, in fact, he has too *little*. Why else would he be so completely focused on himself? We are back again to our distinction between having a strong self-esteem and being self-involved or self-centered. This is a very important issue to understand.

The woman who is preoccupied with her appearance, the man who is forever telling stories in which he emerges as the hero, the person who bores you by going on and on about his or her operation—all of these are examples of people who are so lacking in self-esteem that they are forced compulsively to pay constant attention to themselves, and sometimes to try to get others to do the same. Their self-esteem is so low that they require reinforcement every living moment. They cannot tolerate another in the limelight. They do not care to listen to other people's stories or other people's problems. When they are not given attention, they have an internal or an external temper tantrum. If external, they rant and rave, becoming inappropriately furious at whoever is around—usually a mate, a partner or their children, but sometimes strangers as well. These are the people who are known as "difficult." If the tantrum is internal, either they have a tremendous, unexpressed rage against those who slighted them, or they turn the rage against themselves, berating themselves mercilessly, becoming depressed about their inadequacy to command the attention they need.

Recently I was on a tour with one such person. He was an intelligent, successful man, but he had to have attention focused on him every moment. As we drove past people going to work, he would say, "Look, the people are going to work." When our guides took us anywhere, he would have a barrage of inane questions for them, and he would hardly listen to the answers. He did not really care about the answers. He only

wanted to speak in order to get attention. The people
on the tour became angrier and angrier at him. There
were all sorts of verbal and nonverbal expressions of
disapproval, as far as could be managed within the
realms of civilized behavior. Our friend was completely
oblivious to all of this. He was *self-centered*; totally focused on himself. But he certainly did not have a high
degree of self-esteem. The people on the tour could not
understand him. I tried to explain to the others that he
was like a small, innocent baby, needing constant attention. He did not mean to annoy anyone; he did not
even realize he was annoying anyone. However, I must
admit that my understanding did not diminish my
hostility toward him.

People like this man have a great deal of trouble
getting along with others. It is impossible to be intimate with them for they are basically incapable of inti-
macy. The mate of such a spouse is usually
tremendously drained by the relationship, and either
withers away or leaves. Self-centered people are able to
give very little and they demand so much that their
company means always having a negative balance of
intake versus output. This is a situation similar to that
of a nation's with a consistently negative trade balance;
eventually this will do it in. So being self-centered does
not mean having a great degree of self-esteem. Actually, it's the opposite.

At this point, it is necessary and important to make
a clear differentiation between an *objective* and a *subjective* view of one's self. You can say objectively to
yourself that you know you are attractive, intelligent,
successful, and likable. But you can *feel* that you are
ugly, stupid, unsuccessful, and unpopular. Self-image is
how you *feel* about yourself subjectively. Strangely
enough, this *feeling* is often very little influenced by
objective reality. I have treated young men who
achieved Phi Beta Kappa at Harvard, but still felt
themselves to be stupid. They rationalized that they got
good grades because they worked harder than anyone
else, rather than because they were bright. And I have

treated models whose pictures were on the cover of *Vogue* who felt themselves to be ugly. They rationalized that their photographs really hid all of their bad features. Similarly, I have known people who were, in fact, not very attractive physically or very intelligent, who imagined themselves to be attractive and intelligent.

Self-esteem is determined largely by our childhood experiences. Negative experiences often have the effect of blocking the process that allows us to accept praise and admiration for our successes. Instead of our being able to enhance our sense of self-esteem, growing with each success, our feeling about ourself stays exactly the same. We treat people who have this problem with psychoanalysis. But I feel that some education about the nature of the process has an impact, too. Once we get over the confusion in our thinking about the issue and make clear in our own minds the distinction between self-esteem and self-centeredness, I think we will cease needing to be so self-effacing. We will be able to do some of the things that enhance our self-esteem, opening doors that allow us to take in appropriate praise from others (as well as from ourselves) for our virtues and accomplishments. This in turn will lead to our being less thin-skinned, less vulnerable to criticism or to the slings and arrows of misfortune. Then we will find that we no longer need to be so self-centered and so obsessed with our own image, since, in fact, our image is growing with each of our accomplishments and with the praise we give ourselves, as well as with the recognition we can now take in freely from others.

CHAPTER 5

Roots of Self-esteem

Probably the most crucial period—in terms of the development of a healthy self-esteem—is the first year of life. At that time, we begin to get a feeling of what we are like. And where do we get this feeling? It results mainly from how we see ourselves reflected in our mother's eyes. Our first feeling about whether we are acceptable, lovable people comes from the gleam in her eye and her utter delight in us. If we receive enough of this kind of maternal response at *this* time, there is very little that can markedly shake our self-esteem. If we don't, then we will probably experience at least some difficulty feeling really good about ourselves, no matter how positive our later experiences are.

Some of us were very lucky; we had mothers who loved being mothers and thought their babies the most wonderful creations in the world. Some of us were not so lucky. We had mothers who did not really choose to be mothers, who got pregnant by accident, not realizing they had the choice *not* to be mothers. There are some of us whose mothers died at our birth, who were shifted from person to person, from institution to institution, from foster home to foster home. There are those of us whose mothers were physically or emotionally ill during the first year of our lives. There are those whose mothers were too preoccupied with husbands or with another child to be able to enjoy us and respond to us as babies. And there are some whose mothers were too self-centered to appreciate another person for himself, seeing a child only as an extension of themselves. (We will deal more fully with this in a later chapter.)

There are many different circumstances that may keep us from getting the proper amount of admiration during this crucial period. Another factor is the presence or absence of others—fathers, grandparents, siblings, maids, nurses—either to take up some of the slack if mother falters (or can be of no help) or even to exert a negative influence if they respond badly to us. If we do not get the admiration we need, we start life with a tremendous handicap, especially in the area of our subjective view of ourselves—our self-image and our self-esteem.

But the ball game isn't over by the end of year one. What happens afterward can have considerable influence either to raise our self-esteem or reduce it even further. There are some mothers who are adept with babies, but have all sorts of problems once the child begins to walk, at around the end of the first year. A baby may seem like a doll or a toy; suckling may represent tremendous fulfillment. Yet, when the infant becomes a more separate person, these mothers may see him as a demanding intruder, rather than as a gratifying toy. If the baby has received a great deal of steady adulation, he may already have enough of a store of self-esteem and be able to survive this without too much damage. If his level was somewhat lower, and the change in the mother's attitude is very abrupt, the child's self-esteem may be damaged.

In this period, the role of the father, grandparents, siblings, etc., can help, harm, or have no effect. These also are people whom we may tend to idealize. If they enjoy our loving them, and they in turn care for us, we may then take into ourselves the parts of them that *we* admire. Then—since these parts become a part of ourselves—we like, admire, and esteem those parts of our-selves.

This process of idealizing people and then taking them into ourselves gives us another opportunity (after the first year of life and continuing thereafter) to add to our feeling of loving and admiring ourselves. So even if we weren't lucky enough to have a good mother or mother surrogate during the first year of life, we have other chances later on to take in good feelings about ourselves. We can truly admire a father, grand-parent, or older sibling. Then, as we move away from close contact with them, we take into ourselves pieces of them that we value; in that way, we get to value ourselves. Most often, this happens to boys who are fortunate enough to have a father around whom they can admire. Eventually, it works out better if the figure we idealize is of our gender, but this isn't necessary. Girls can admire fathers or older brothers and take in aspects of them, and boys can take in aspects of moth-ers or older sisters.

During adolescence, we are apt to admire and to ab-sorb qualities in teachers or heroes. Those of us who lacked sufficient admiration from our mothers during our first year, and did not have a father or older sibling we could truly idealize, tend to develop, during child-hood, with a very low self-esteem. In this period, we can try to repair the damage by idealizing another adult figure—a coach or a teacher or an aunt or an uncle. Or we can develop a crush on or worship some-one in adolescence, and even during our adult life. Babe Ruth, who was an orphan and was brought up in Catholic institutions, clearly admired and idealized some of the priests who taught him. He was able to achieve success as an adult, though he tended to be grandiose and unstable.

All through our lives, we attach ourselves to people we admire, and then we identify with traits of theirs. In this way, we get to like ourselves since we have be-come like some of the people we saw objectively and liked, and also tended to idealize. If, during childhood, there is no one around of the same sex for us to admire, we may admire and internalize a member of the opposite sex to a very great degree. Then we may have problems about our gender identity, our feeling of security in being masculine or feminine. I have a patient who got little admiration from her mother and tremendously idealized her father. He admired her mind but was not responsive to her as a girl and a daughter. Eventually, she followed him into his profession. Though she is beautiful and has a lovely figure, her body-image is that of a six-foot, 180-pound man like her father. She sees herself subjectively, differently from the objective truth.

I want you to visualize the fluid, dynamic picture of how the self-esteem system starts and continues, how different people and different experiences constantly feed the storehouse or drain it. This process continues throughout our developing years, through adolescence and into our adult lives. In general, though, the earlier in our lives, the greater is the impact of these combined forces.

This does not mean that in adolescence the impact is not important. As a matter of fact, the reflection of the parent of the opposite sex can have a considerable impact on our sexual development. A father who can acknowledge, without shame or anxiety, his admiration for his blossoming adolescent daughter can certainly reinforce the positive image she will have of herself as a sexual woman. And a mother can perceive her son as a sexual male. Many parents are embarrassed by their normal sexual responses to their adolescent children of the opposite sex. To avoid embarrassment about what they may feel are unnatural or incestuous feelings, they may be loath to express genuine admiration to their sons or daughters. Some parents are so uncomfortable with their adolescent children of the opposite sex that they may cut themselves off emotionally from them. On the other hand, parents of the same sex regularly can be expected to experience some degree of competitive feeling toward their adolescent children.

This may influence them—without their awareness of it—to be critical in areas of physical appearance or of their children's attempts to present themselves as more sexual beings. These two factors, among many, can have a strong influence on the growth or diminution of the adolescent's self-image.

If mother is critical every time her daughter puts on lipstick or wears a tight sweater, and father turns away to avoid his embarrassment, the daughter's physical self-image will certainly not be enhanced. And she may expect her boyfriends to react negatively to her expressions of sexuality. But if both parents admire her developing womanhood, she is more likely to anticipate positive responses from her boyfriends. Admiring peer responses, or the lack of them, can also exert an influence.

One of my patients told me that, in her adolescence, every time she put on makeup or tightly fitting clothes, her mother would say she looked like a whore and her father would say she had no taste. Though she persisted, and often got positive and admiring responses from boys at school, she was never sure whether they were admiring her or mocking her. Many adult women are ambivalent over their choice of clothes and have tremendous difficulty in making their selection. One of my patients feels she looks either like a dowdy old woman or a prostitute. She is unable to experience a middle position—of being attractive, but not a sexual object.

Teenagers complimented by their parents will be able to withstand even cruel adolescent taunts. An example of the reverse situation is another patient of mine who was always ridiculed by her mother because of a rather prominent nose. Discovering that her male classmates had dubbed her "The Nose," she was so mortified that she went into a serious withdrawal from her peer group, despite having been one of the most popular, attractive girls in her class.

This dynamic continuum in the self-esteem starts in the first weeks of life, and continues throughout the rest of our lives. Different figures in the environment will play into it—not family figures alone. And, since more Americans have been brought up to be self-effacing than self-centered, the chances are that our models will be modest and self-effacing and that we will tend to follow their example. Those of us who had very self-centered parents might not have been any more fortunate; those parents probably would have wanted to steal the show and might have put down *our* efforts to get attention.

Reactions of peers, teachers, religious figures, etc., can contribute significantly. I have a friend who was shifted from one school to another during her childhood. Children are often critical and hurtful to a stranger, and my friend was often treated as an intruder in already well-established groups. This repeated rejection by a succession of peers created an insecurity—especially in groups—in my friend and certainly lowered her self-esteem. She recalls that each time she moved from one school to another, she had to master a whole new way of doing things—from how and where to hang up coats to a different method of long division. Though she is an exceptionally bright woman, she was always viewed as stupid by her new classmates. This subjective view of her lack of intelligence persisted, despite academic honors and graduate degrees.

Of course, adult success—intellectual, social, and sexual—can have a bearing on our image of ourselves. But I am more impressed by the lack of change in self-image despite outstanding adult success. Going back to my friend, her early image of herself died very very hard, all objective evidence to the contrary. Here again we must clearly distinguish between our *objective* view of ourselves and our *self-image*, or our *subjective* view of ourselves. My friend knew intellectually that she had to be bright because of the many outside confirmations—in college, in graduate school, and in her profession. But her inner view of herself was still very much molded by her childhood, by her early classmates' reaction to her as stupid.

In my emphasis on the persistence of both positive and negative self-images from our childhood, I do not mean to imply that our adult experiences have no bearing on our self-image. Adult success that brings admiration certainly can and does help. However, for many of us—who cannot take in too much praise from ourselves or from others—such success does not have as much impact as one would think it should have. One of the most disastrous effects on our life experiences, especially rooted in parental disapproval of our attempts to feel good about ourselves, is that we may be incapable of taking in merited admiration in our adult life. We are not only damaged from having received an insufficient amount of praise along the way, but we also find it hard to change our initial low self-esteem because of these blocks.

I hope I have given you a picture of the development of the self-esteem system, beginning at birth and continuing throughout our lives. The response to us by our mothers in the first year is perhaps the most crucial, but a succession of different people—fathers, grandparents, siblings, teachers, peers, and others—whom we can idealize and internalize produces a dynamic continuum that adds or detracts from our self-esteem. But even very late in our lives, our self-esteem can change, not only through a succession of positive experiences, but also—as hopefully through this book—by our understanding of the factors that have affected us and are continuing to do so.

Lately, in sophisticated psychoanalytic circles, there has been much more emphasis on the factor of the internalization of the psychoanalyst by the patient as the means by which damage to the self-image is repaired. In former days, there was a tendency to discount this factor as an important therapeutic force. Analysts used to like to think that they were faceless, mechanical technicians who brought about change in their patients through the precision of their interpretations. The idea that they, too, were human beings, possessing unique personalities with whom the patient could identify and then internalize, was rejected as sentimental and unscientific. Recent work, notably by Dr. Kohut and some of his followers, has placed a good deal more emphasis on the personality of the therapist and the internalization of certain qualities of the therapist as, at times, being the major force in a patient's change, especially if the patient's problem was related to a damaged self-image.

We understand now how important a role in building up our self-esteem is played by the internalization of qualities of people that we idealize. This is especially true if these people respond positively to our idealization of them, and enjoy the process. A model for this would be the supposedly typical situation of the boy who thinks his dad is "the greatest guy in the world," and whose dad is proud of his son's being "a chip off the old block." If this can be such a splendid way of taking in qualities we idealize and then loving ourselves because *we* now possess them, in what better situation would such a process occur than in the patient-therapist relationship?

Why psychotherapy works has always been somewhat of a mystery. When people who engage in studies on this issue come to conclusions, they usually decide that what works depends not so much on the training or the theoretical stance of the therapist but on his or her personality. They have found that therapy works when the therapist and patient share the common belief that the therapist has access to a special knowledge about the patient that will make the patient well. Whether the therapist is an analyst, a witch doctor, an astrologer, or a behavior therapist seems to make less difference than the strength of the therapist's personality, his own conviction about the correctness and efficacy of his treatment method, and the patient's belief in him. These findings certainly seem to fit in well with the theory that the crucial factor in therapy is the patient's internalizing qualities of an idealized therapist.

The internalization leads to an increase in self-esteem. Since, in my opinion, self-esteem is the pivotal issue in our feeling of well-being, it follows that those patient-therapist combinations that result in this process work, and those that don't do not.

My own clinical experience has certainly borne out this conclusion. During the course of my career, I have followed several different theoretical systems. The way I treat a patient today is radically different from the way I treated patients twenty-five or thirty years ago. Still, many of the patients I treated then seemed to have improved considerably. Some of them still send me Christmas cards or call when they are in town. Yet my method of treatment at that time is now largely out-of-date and not used by me today. What made them better must have been something in the personal transaction between myself and them. Some of them, who have themselves become psychoanalysts, have confirmed this assumption. Many of them clearly admired me and idealized me, and *I* was certainly delighted with this view of me and responded in kind to them. Probably what made them so much better (and in many the improvement was striking) was not the brilliance of my interpretations but simply the process of their idealization of me. Taking in certain qualities of mine and liking themselves better, they then raised their own level of self-esteem. This rise in their view of themselves enabled them to succeed professionally, socially, and sexually where they used to fail, and also enabled them to bear unpleasant happenings with more equanimity.

Recently I saw a patient after a lapse of twenty years. When I first knew her, she had such a low opinion of herself that she had never even been out on a date. Subsequently she married a fine man, was very happy in her marriage and in her profession, and had two splendid children. She had no serious emotional problems until her husband died suddenly of a heart attack. She came to see me on two occasions for some support, but soon was able to weather even this tragedy in her life without further need for me. It seems clear that the major contributor to her rise in self-esteem was the process of idealizing and then internalizing qualities of mine. The consequent rise in her self-esteem enabled her to enjoy a happy life, and then even to survive the blow of her husband's death without a severe depletion of her self-esteem.

CHAPTER 6

Grandiosity and Its Relationship to Self-esteem

When we talk about grandiosity, we must begin with the idea that it is a normal stage of development during the first months of life. The infant is, or should be, at the center of his world. His environment is limited by the development of his eyes, ears, and brain, so obviously he cannot know that there is a whole world going on out there that does not include him. His world is made up of himself, his bodily sensations, and his mother. At first he does not see his mother as a separate entity from himself. During the first few months of his life, he experiences her as part of himself, a part that is almost totally under his control. If his mother is very close to him—almost joined with him as a normal mother is during the first months of a baby's life—then she will be tremendously responsive to him. From subtle little signs, she will know that her baby is hungry, that he is sleepy, that he is cold. Often the baby will not even have to cry or send out a specific signal before his wish is granted. No wonder he feels like an omnipotent little god at the center of his universe, whose only contact, his mother, is totally at his beck and call. Along with being a little emperor, he is also a little tyrant. When his wishes are not fulfilled, he yells and cries and kicks and screams; he would practically destroy his world if he had the physical capability. This is a stage of openly displayed grandiosity. The baby is a demanding and tyrannical emperor over his entire kingdom.

If we are lucky and have a mother who is closely involved with us as babies, reasonably fulfilling our need to be grandiose tyrants, in time we will be able to yield to the reality that neither the world nor our mother is totally at our command. If she is a "good-enough" mother, she will provide optimum frustration for us, as well as optimum need-fulfillment. As our senses and our bodies develop, we will begin to be able to tolerate waiting a while for our bottle, doing without her for a few hours, not having her come to us immediately at our very first cry. Gradually we will get used to the idea that we are not really the kings of the universe. As our awareness develops, our appreciation that the world is bigger than ourselves and our mothers will begin to seep through to us. If our frustration is gradual enough, we will be able to accept, without too much of a problem, that there is a whole world around us that we cannot control.

But at a certain stage of our development, we do have a need to experience the world in this grandiose way. In many cultures, the baby is strapped to the mother's back—literally joined to her—for the first year or two. In the world of one hundred years ago, when most families were intact, mothers rarely worked or even left the house without taking the baby with them. Most babies received the kind of total attention they required. Over the past decades, the world—and perhaps especially our country—has undergone enormous changes in the stability of the family in the closeness of the mother-child relationship. To one degree or another, there are many babies who pass through this stage of infantile grandiosity without satisfaction of all their needs to be tyrannical emperors. This was true, of course, during all ages for children whose mothers died at birth, or who were abandoned or put into institutions, or whose mothers were not at their disposal for a variety of reasons. All these situations still exist, but even when a mother is at home and is physically available, she may not have the disposition to be involved with her baby in this particular merged way at this important time of his life.

The fact is that many of us are left with some frustrations stemming from the amount of grandiosity we experienced at that age-appropriate time. From this frustration come fantasies, especially in our childhood, about being rich and famous and powerful, being able to get all of our needs met instantly, and being in control of the world. These fantasies are also frequently accompanied by tyrannical dreams of punishing our enemies or any people who stand in the way of our realizing our wishes. I think a reason for the popularity of the motion picture, *The Godfather*, was that it portrayed people with the power to get immediately whatever they wanted and to destroy anyone who got in their way. Such people, at least as they were portrayed, are the ultimate, omnipotent, grandiose tyrants, above the law, with the whole world at their disposal. But almost everyone has had a fantasy of being a king or an absolute dictator, totally in command of his entire world. These fantasies are often quite charming in children; some of us continue to be conscious of them in our adult life.

But before we continue with the results of thwarted infantile grandiosity, let us explore another state of affairs that can lead to difficulty in the area of grandiosity—the child not receiving optimum frustration from his parents or his environment. If the child at age two or seven, or fourteen or thirty-nine, is treated by his environment as if he really is an omnipotent ruler, then he will persist in his unrealistic belief that he is the emperor of the universe, instead of gradually relinquishing his grandiosity. We observe this phenomenon in babies whose mothers do not let them go soon enough. We often see it in babies and children who are especially rich or beautiful or intelligent or talented. Instead of being treated like other children and having to accept the fact that their power is limited, they are deified. We see it in child prodigies like Oscar Levant or child movie stars like Judy Garland, who had so much psychological difficulty in their adult lives. We also see it in real-life little princes and princesses, who in fact often do become outrageous tyrants as kings or queens. Henry VIII is a vivid example of this. When one of his wives failed to please him, he had her beheaded. Marie Antoinette is another example. When told that her subjects had no bread to eat, she is supposed to have said, "Then let them eat cake." We can develop problems about grandiosity from two sources—one, if we did not have our appropriate need for grandiosity satisfied during the early months of life, and two, if we were treated as special god-like people at any age past the first year or two of life.

As an example of the latter problem, Peggy all but really believed she was a princess. At least, she thought of herself as someone very special. Her family came close to being royalty in the medium-sized American city in which she was raised. Her father may have been the richest man—very much involved in civic affairs and respected by all as a benefactor and philanthropist. Peggy was brought up with many servants and luxuries, but as opulent as her home was financially, it was as impoverished emotionally. Her father—in contrast to his public image—was an omnipotent, nasty, irrational tyrant at home. He deprecated Peggy's mother constantly, as well as Peggy and her sister and brother. But he also controlled them by assuring them they would never want for anything because of his great wealth.

Peggy grew up feeling she belonged to a "royal" family, that her connection to her father assured her of the life of luxury she deserved. She never did well at school, despite a high intelligence, but she was very popular with men. She did very little work until her middle twenties, spending her time dating men of a certain princely image—wealthy, successful, well-bred, and educated at the best schools. Several of these men fell in love with her and proposed, but she became disenchanted with them all. Unconsciously, she compared them to her father and none of them matched her idealized image of him. The problem that brought Peggy into treatment was one of alternating rages and depressions when things did not go her way. She maintained her grandiose image of being a princess and could not tolerate the smallest frustration in her life. She suffered great humiliation at the most minor slight, and would have the grown-up equivalent of a two-year-old temper tantrum. To get over her problem, eventually she had to accept the fact that she was *not* a princess or a privileged person, that she was as subject as any one else to the vicissitudes of life and fortune.

Giving up a grandiose view of one's self is not easy. First of all, admitting to such a view is difficult. Those who do admit it are not apt to let go of it easily. Like Peggy, usually they had some childhood experiences that enhanced their grandiosity—being wealthy or beautiful or bright, or very talented in the arts. Singled out for special attention, they became accustomed to expecting the world to treat them as special.

Len, a young man I have treated, is an unusually gifted actor. His first two roles of any importance on the Broadway stage resulted in rave reviews and nominations for acting awards. In his middle twenties, he was one of the brightest stars in the theater. The sky seemed to be the limit as to how far and how fast he would climb in his profession. Since his rise was based on hard work and mastery of the acting craft, rather than on good looks or a trendy personality, there was no reason for thinking he was a flash in the pan. He had worked and studied and now his efforts were properly rewarded. A serious actor, he played many different kinds of roles, from leading men to low comics to old men. If ever there was a basis for belief in a performer's continued success, it seemed to be so in his case. But along with this sudden recognition, there came an enormous increase in his grandiosity. Believing quite appropriately that he was a very fine actor, he also began to believe that he was leagues ahead of most of his contemporaries, and that his appearance should invariably be greeted by recognition, homage to his skill, and almost immediate acceptance of himself in any role that interested him.

This kind of belief is common among actors. I have treated several theater people and known many others personally. Rarely have I encountered one who did not feel secretly that he or she was the greatest of all time. One of my patients, who had starred in high-school plays, had a career consisting of a walk-on without even a line in an off-off Broadway show. She was convinced that, given a break or two, she would have been the world's greatest actress. Another patient, a veteran of a bit part in a Broadway show, always referred to and comported herself as if she were star. Actors get a great deal of attention, recognition, admiration, and applause. They tend—as do many critics—to use superlatives to describe one another's performances. Most of us cringe—during the Academy Award presentations or the Toni Award telecasts—at all the adulation that the stars heap upon one another and all the phony humility and modesty they show when receiving their prizes. The praise may be merited, but the hypocrisy revolts us.

Returning to our talented young friend, Len, he quickly developed a very grandiose view of himself. This encompassed contempt for other performers not quite as talented or as fortunate as himself. Along with this, however, came a tremendous anxiety when he did receive praise or awards. This anxiety was not phony or a product of false modesty. On the other hand, it was clearly connected with his fear of his grandiosity getting completely out of control and the danger of becoming really megalomaniacal. When he received genuine praise, he found it very difficult to take it in. Along with this, he became rather unbearable when he was with his friends. The slightest hint that he was not the world's greatest authority on acting and on everything else in the world produced a narcissistic rage, equivalent to a temper tantrum. Many times this rage was expressed outwardly; he became hostile and obnoxious at parties. This, in turn, produced in him feelings of shame and humiliation afterwards. Often the rage was internalized; some slight, enlarged from a molehill into a mountain, would send him into a terrible depression.

At auditions, he would have a difficult time with his feelings. Frequently, he would start by feeling the part was beneath him, although occasionally he was trying out for a part that he felt merited his ability. But then he would consider the possibility of rejection—even for an inferior role. The thought of this would so infuriate him that he could hardly control his rage when he appeared for the audition. Then, of course, most of the time he *was* rejected for the role. Plays are not cast on the basis of talent alone. Often the producer has in mind a certain type which the actor may not fit, for a variety of reasons. Len's rage at rejection was monumental, as was his vilification of the people who rejected him. This was invariably followed by a complete loss of self-confidence, a feeling that he was really no good at all, and serious questions about his career choice. If he wasn't picked, then perhaps he wasn't the greatest. And if he wasn't the greatest, he was nothing. Len's reactions were a classic example of the so-called "Hero-Zero split." If Len wasn't a hero, a grandiose, larger-than-life success, then he was a zero, a total failure. He had trouble experiencing himself as anything in between. People whose grandiosity has been overindulged by the environment often have this problem.

How did Len solve this dilemma? How did he deal with this grandiosity and its pitfalls? The last time I saw him, he told me he had been reading biographies of some of the stars. Melvin Douglas was not considered a serious actor until he was in his forties; he got the part opposite Greta Garbo in *Ninotchka* only because William Powell, who was slated for the part, became ill. Marie Dressler was a failure in her fifties until she caught on suddenly. Wallace Beery went absolutely nowhere until he reached his fifties.

Len began to see that even the biggest stars had had

their ups and downs. He began to realize that, even though he was good, he was not necessarily the greatest. And even being one of the greatest did not guarantee instant or continued success and approval. So he has begun to scale himself down to life-size. His expectations of himself and the responses to him are no longer grandiose, but much more realistic. He realizes that, even if he may, in fact, be the best actor auditioning for a part, he is not *so* great that invariably he will be chosen for it. There is a flattening out of both the degree of his grandiosity and the degree of his narcissistic rage. He has come down from Mount Olympus and joined the human race. He still has an appreciation of his talents, but no longer a grandiose view of himself. And he is much happier and less prone to fits of depression.

These depressions, including suicide attempts, are common among performers. Not so long ago, we were confronted with the tragedy of talented, young Freddie Prinze who killed himself at the beginning of a promising career. According to his friend, Tony Orlando, one of the main reasons for Prinze's suicide was because he wanted to become a "legend" like Jimmy Dean, in order to achieve a kind of immortality. In my view, the reason for so many depressions and suicides among entertainers—as well as among other kinds of stars—is that they get so much admiration and adulation that their grandiosity is inflated. Then any small slight becomes unbearable. The narcissistic rage that is evoked is turned against the self; not infrequently depressions, including suicidal ones, result. The treatment of people with this problem is to make them aware of their grandiosity. This is no easy task for an analyst; they are sensitive to any slight, easily humiliated by any suggestion that their view of themselves is inflated. Often they become quite angry, feeling the analyst does not appreciate them and is putting them down. If this process can be handled with delicacy and tact, the patient can begin to experience himself as more life-sized—good but not the greatest of all time. Once this has been accomplished, the terrible highs and lows begin to fade. The patient experiences himself more as a human being, rather than as some kind of god. His expectations—of himself and of the responses to him from the people around him—become more realistic. Then he can take adversity without perceiving it as a personal wound to his grandiosity, but just as a regular occurrence that all human beings must face at some times in their lives.

This sort of problem is especially poignant in people who enjoy tremendous and exalted status at some time in life, and then lose it completely. The aging athlete is a striking example of a person who literally goes from the greatest to nothing as the years impair his ability to maintain the level of his performance. We have all felt saddened at seeing the star baseball player or basketball player who goes on one year too long. That last year is an embarrassment to the fans and a humiliation to himself. We admire athletes like Joe DiMaggio, who knew enough to quit while he was still in his prime.

There was an excellent movie called *I Never Sang for My Father*, which depicted a complicated father-son relationship. My own relationship with my father was so complex that years and years of psychoanalysis never clarified it. It was only a year ago, when he died slowly over a six-month period at the age of eighty-four, that with the help of Dr. Kohut's work on narcissism, I was able to begin to unravel some of its subtleties.

I never sang for my father. We rarely communicated to each other more than a few perfunctory sentences over fifty-three years of my life. We practically never did anything together—not even a movie or a ball game. Consciously, I hated and feared him throughout my childhood, and disliked him intensely throughout all of my adult life. I never did anything for him, yet everything I ever did was for his and his father's approval. My paternal grandfather *did* dote on me and made me feel I was the world's greatest genius. After my grandfather died when I was fourteen, I spent most of my life seeking my father's approval, trying to get some nod of recognition from him. He never once in his life called me Richard. He never called me anything. I had a constant fantasy that one day he would put his arm around my shoulder and call me Richard. The fantasy never came true.

My father was a very successful doctor. He never attended high school or college. By passing equivalency examinations, he went practically from grammar school to one of the finest medical schools in the country. He always told stories of how he was a self-made man. He never told them directly to me, but I was present in the room. My father was a tremendous braggart. He would speak of how he walked ten miles through the snow to save a sick child. He told how seven professors of medicine had missed a diagnosis, and how *he* had identified the illness from across a large ward. To a child like myself, he was a very easy person to idealize. In my mind—without realizing it consciously—I had made him into a god. He was perfect, omniscient, and immortal. Consciously, I hated him because either he ignored me or belittled me. The very distance he put between himself and me increased my idealization of him. After age twelve, I had no belief in God. I did not need it. My father was God.

I know now that I became a doctor in order to please him. It didn't work. When I became a psychiatrist, he said that *he*, an internist, was then and always had been a much better psychiatrist than I would ever be. Besides, he said, psychiatrists were the garbage collectors of the medical profession. When my first article was published in a medical journal—an article on neurology rather than on psychiatry—his single comment was that it was only three pages long. He locked up one of the books I wrote so that my mother would not see it because it contained some material about sex. All this built up my idealization of him. Although consciously I hated him, I saw him as all the more powerful and superhuman. I redoubled my efforts to attain his approval, but never with any results.

When my father had a heart attack at age eighty-four, at first I absolutely refused to believe it was real. I had built up in my mind the idea of his immortality. As he began to fail, I continued for as long as I could to deny it. And I began to discover that along with denying his mortality I had simultaneously denied my own, and that a great deal of the grandiosity I had projected on to him was also a part of my own. Finally I had to accept the fact that he was failing rapidly. Some of my colleagues pushed me hard to attempt one real, honest communication with him before he died. I resisted this idea with all my might. Since some of these colleagues had been my patients—and I had pushed them to similar confrontations with their parents with important results—finally I had to yield.

I was extremely nervous when I entered my father's living room. I had no script. I didn't know what I wanted to say. Nevertheless, I knew I had to try. I asked my mother to leave us alone—saying that for the first time in my life I wanted to talk to my father.

"Pop," I said, "there is one thing I have always wanted from you, and that is recognition of my professional accomplishment."

"There is only one way you could have gotten that," he said with his usual candor. "That is if you had become professor of psychiatry at Harvard Medical School."

"But, Pop," I said. "I wouldn't take that job if they paid me a million dollars a year. What I do as a psychoanalyst is infinitely more creative and challenging. And I teach seasoned professionals, not medical students."

"Well, that's the way it is," he said.

At least now I knew. There was no way I would ever please my father! No matter how perfect I became in my own eyes, I would never be anyone in his. I had to face his death and his lack of immortality, as well as my own inability to join with him on Mt. Olympus. My idealization and projection of grandiosity onto him was over. My own grandiosity—trying to be the perfect enough person for him to accept—was also over. He died shortly thereafter. Along with his death, my own sense of grandiosity and immortality began to die. I started to see his imperfections and for the first time, on a deep level, to admit my own.

The result of working through these issues was spectacular for me. Now that I was not a god, I no longer had to be perfect. I no longer expected Olympian performances from myself in the office, on the tennis court, or in bed. I no longer chastised myself every time I came up a bit short of my grandiose expectations of myself. Allowing myself to be human and fallible and mortal was a tremendous relief from the tension of seeking perfection. It also meant that I could accept rejections and slights from other people, and misfortunes that occurred by chance. I ceased to be so sensitive that I would be either enraged or depressed when things did not go my way.

When my father died, my grandiosity died with him. Thinking one is a god may make life dramatic, but seeing oneself as a human being is much more comfortable, much easier. Also, I am not writing this book for Pop. I'm writing it for you and for me.

To return to our discussion of our grandiose fantasies, as I said above, most of us have fantasies of being the most beautiful or most powerful or wealthiest person in the world. If we can acknowledge these fantasies, as most of us can and do in childhood, we may not have any particular problem with them. However, if we have been especially deprived of feeling grandiose during our early months of life, or have had our grandiosity overindulged at some later point, these fantasies may become threatening to us. We must remember that they are fantasies in which our power is used not only to gratify our every whim immediately but also to destroy anyone who comes between us and our gratification. If we are not frightened by our ability to get whatever we wish, we may well be frightened of our destructiveness. This causes most of us to bury our fantasies, to push them out of range of our awareness. It also accounts, in larger measure, for the tremendous social disapproval we heap upon someone else who tends to be grandiose. If we are so afraid of our own grandiosity, we will be threatened by that of others, and we will tend to put them down and ridicule them when they begin to display it.

But the most important result of our fear of our own grandiosity—even if it is restricted to seemingly harmless fantasies—is that we become frightened whenever we are given deserved praise. Instead of being able to take in some recognition of our ability or attractiveness or performance, we become uncomfortable with it out of all proportion. I remember a party when a friend of mine introduced me to a friend of hers in the most laudatory kind of manner. I became so uncomfortable that I said, "Laura, please do me a favor. Say some rotten things about me, quick." Laura, partly with tongue in cheek, obliged me all too readily. I was taken aback, but my anxiety was vastly relieved. I remember, another time, complaining to a lover that she did not really love or appreciate me. She turned to me tenderly and told me exactly what I had thought I wanted to hear—that she loved me very much and thought very highly of me. Instead of being delighted, I became so anxious that I felt like hiding my face and running out of the room. Have you had experiences like this? Do you feel good when people compliment you, or do you feel anxious and upset?

If we examine the reason we have this strange reaction of anxiety rather than pleasure when someone says something we think we would like to hear, the only sound explanation is that it threatens our grandiosity. But if we carry this argument further, we can see that we are forced to avoid the very things that we need the most—the compliments and praises that would build our self-esteem. The culprit is our fear of our grandiosity if we should accept them.

More specifically, what is it we fear? Why are we so afraid to admit our grandiose fantasies, or to take in a merited compliment, or even, in some instances, to allow ourselves to succeed? We fear that if we let in anything good, we will escalate this into being grandiose. And then what? First of all, there is a fear of vanity, which might be followed by the disapproval of our fellows. And then there is a fear that the grandiosity would turn us into a grown-up version of that infant tyrant, that we would go around cutting off people's heads, literally or figuratively. This would be contrary to our moral standards, and might ultimately lead to rejection and punishment. Besides, suppose we allowed ourselves to indulge our feeling of grandiosity, think of facing the tremendous fall from the heights, a fall that might lead to embarrassment, humiliation, or, even worse, self-destruction.

One of my patients was promoted to a very good position. She had this dream: "My boyfriend and I were scaling the World Trade Center (as someone had done in reality the week before her dream). We were almost up to the top when, all of a sudden, I slipped and I started plummeting toward the ground. I looked up at my boyfriend. On seeing me fall, he decided that life wasn't worth living without me and he started to fall along with me. All of a sudden, I noticed he had wings. So, instead of falling to his death along with me, he went into a beautiful glide and flew away."

This is a classic dream about grandiosity. In her unconscious, my patient's promotion was escalated by her into the equivalent of scaling the tallest building in the world. Then she began to fall from these heights. (In reality, she had gone into a deep depression after her promotion.) In the dream, she tried to recoup her grandiosity by feeling she was so indispensible that life without her would be worthless to her boyfriend. But this attempt at grandiosity also failed. Instead of committing suicide at her death (much like the wives of kings jumping into the funeral pyre), her boyfriend blithely glided away. Once more she was left with egg on her face—mortified and humiliated even as she was plunging to her death.

This dream demonstrates the punishment for the sin of vanity, which is, in fact, part of many primitive beliefs. It is also interwoven into the *kineahora*, which is believed—consciously or unconsciously—by many contemporary Jews. The idea is that one should not say anything too flattering about one's self or about a friend in order to prevent some powerful and jealous God-like being from throwing down the equivalent of a thunderbolt and destroying the person who has been praised. If your friend has a new baby, you should not extol the child's beauty too much without saying *kineahora* to ward off evil or something bad (like a fatal illness) will befall her.

I remember once, in a therapy group, some of my Jewish patients discussing the *kineahora* and its effect on holding down their joy, putting a damper on their good feelings. One of them turned to me and said, "Say, do the Italians have anything like that?"

"Of course," I said. "We call it *malocchio*, or evil eye. It's the same idea. If you look at something or someone too favorably, the evil eye will destroy the object of your admiration. There are even special talismans like red peppers to ward off the evil eye."

One of the men in the group was a black man. "Tell me, Jim, do black people have the same kind of magical thinking about enjoying something good too much?"

Jim thought for a while. "No," he said, "I can't think of anything like that. Maybe it's because nothing good has ever happened for us blacks."

To recapitulate, we are likely to have problems about grandiosity if, first, our normal needs for grandiosity were not indulged during our early months of life; and/or, second, if we were overindulged and treated in an inappropriately grandiose manner at any time of our life—either in childhood or in adult life—after our first year of life. Either of these two experiences—and many of us are subjected to at least the first, if not both—leave us with a tendency to think of ourselves in a grandiose way. For most of us, since we aren't movie stars, athletic heroes, beauty queens, or intellectual giants, our grandiosity is expressed mainly in fantasies of being all-powerful. With the fantasy of power comes also the power to destroy. Even though most of us are conscious of these fantasies at some time in childhood, our fear of loss of control of our primitive, tyrannical sadism, our fear of ridicule and humiliation, or simply our fear of falling from the heights of our grandeur causes most of us to suppress these fantasies. But these dreams of glory, though mostly outside of our awareness, still exert a tremendous influence on us. It is our fear of these fantasies that constricts us, that makes us play down our successes and joys, that renders us unable to take in appropriate compliments that are merited. These fantasies are the culprits that prevent us from taking in the very buildings blocks we need for our self-esteem. Besides this, the fear connected with these fantasies can actually keep some of us from succeeding to the degree of which we are capable in reality. We will examine some of the ways we defend ourselves against the fears of these fantasies and the great cost of it to ourselves. Then we will try to see what we can do to change this process, so we will be able to succeed, take in the praise for our success, and derive a consequent growth in our self-esteem.

CHAPTER 7

Defense Against Fears of Grandiosity

There are two classic defenses against our fears of grandiosity. One is called the *horizontal split* and the other is called the *vertical split* .

The person with the horizontal split in his self-esteem is a person who just pushes it down. He is overly modest, self-effacing, and constantly puts himself down. He cannot take a compliment, is very quick to acknowledge his deficiencies but never his virtues, never tries to get attention through dress, speech, or talent, and hides his accomplishments. Are you one of these? Possibly. Most of us tend in this direction, finding it difficult to take in any plaudits or successes in order to increase our self-esteem, or even acknowledge a little healthy admiration from *ourselves*. That is the *horizontal split*, not really complicated.

The *vertical split* isn't complicated either. The person with the vertical split is constantly "coming on," trying to get people's attention. He tells anecdotes and jokes, utilizes his talent to get recognition (like my writing this book), constantly tries to get people to give him approval and admiration. But even though he goes after admiration, he has a vertical "gardol" shield. He blocks it out completely. It is as if that person striving so for admiration is completely disowned, not remotely connected with him. Compulsively, he keeps trying to get attention and often succeeds, but it adds not one iota to his self-esteem. Is this you? Possibly, if you tend to be a more outgoing and exhibitionistic person. Most people—at least in America—are less likely to suffer the vertical split. The reason some people tend to be exhibitionistic and others self-effacing is not really clear; it is probably partly hereditary or constitutional. Even at day one, some babies lie quietly in their cribs, while others squirm around, screaming. Also, there may be environmental reasons pertaining to role-models, the people in our families whom we tend to internalize and make into parts of ourselves. Certainly there are exceptions, but why are most Italians outgoing and most Swedes introverted and self-effacing? The answer is probably a combination of hereditary and constitutional factors and identifications with role-models in childhood and adolescence.

Actually there is seldom a complete demarcation between these splits. In many of us, a mixture of both occurs. But as a result, whether it is horizontally or vertically, our poor self-esteem gets either *pushed down* or *pushed away* from us, so that we never have enough of a good feeling about ourselves.

Thus we protect ourselves against those grandiose fantasies which we fear so dreadfully. We are so frightened and ashamed of these fantasies of being the greatest that we defend ourselves too strongly against them, not letting in any praise, or risking a rise in self-esteem. Wanting to be a hero may lead to grandiosity or humiliation, so we'd rather play it safe by being the zero. But underneath we need to and want to be heroes, and when our virtues are *not* acknowledged, we are very easily hurt. Our vertical and horizontal splits don't keep us from being very sensitive to criticism. On the other hand, since our self-esteem has already been so pushed out or pushed down by our selves, if anyone else takes a crack at it, that is the final blow. We just can't take it, so we have a temper tantrum. We become furious, either at other people or at ourselves. This is one of the most common dynamics in depression and in suicide.

Even on a smaller scale, we can go on feeling badly if we react this way to negative comment. Our only escape is to try to be so powerful, to inspire so much fear, that no one will dare to criticize us. Some of us surround ourselves with yes-men and worshipers. Even then we will be constantly anxious because of our precarious position. Anything or anybody can come along and knock us off our perch, and reality is bound to frustrate or disappoint us at least once in a while. Then we will be either furious or self-destructive. A classic illustration of this is the person who cannot tolerate being in a traffic jam. He starts honking his horn and cursing the other drivers, or else he berates himself for his stupidity in taking this particular road. People with this problem of needing to be perfect must have a constant level of anxiety because their self-esteem system is so dependent upon outside forces beyond their control. The anxiety may be so constant that it becomes a way of life; the person just thinks he is that way normally.

Dolly had a problem studying for exams. She was forty, a graduate student who had entered a new profession at the age of thirty-five. She had been very successful in her former field. Starting out as an opera singer, she had made a name for herself, and then gone on to become an operatic stage manager. Here, too, she was very much of a success. But just as she was about to reach the very top, she had left the field and become a vocal coach. Here, too, she was an immediate success. Once again, as she was about to achieve recognition, she decided to get into the field of speech therapy; she went to graduate school while simultaneously starting a small practice. Her practice grew by leaps and bounds; she was marvelous at making contact with people. Clients referred their friends and relatives to her. In a little while, she had more clients and was making more money than many of her teachers. But while she was maintaining a small private clientele, she found herself unable to read the material of speech therapy—to study the literature, to learn the concepts, to read the books. When she went into her examinations, she was in a panic. She had not really learned the theoretical material and she did poorly.

Have you ever had a typical examination dream? It is one of the most common dreams. In a recurring one of mine, I find myself in a school about to take a very important examination on which my future depends. I arrive in the room, sit down, and receive my examination paper. The subject of the examination is the Lithuanian language. I do not know a word of Lithuanian, have never ever heard one word of it uttered, and have never taken a course in it. Oh God!

That is practically the way Dolly feels when she takes an examination. Of course, she has a certain familiarity with the field, but very little with the specific readings and theories about which she is examined. She tries to "wing it," "bullshit" her way through the test, but she is terrified that she will be discovered as a fraud, exposed and humiliated. She panics, does even worse than she would ordinarily do, and, in fact, her fantasized humiliation becomes a reality, a self-fulfilling prophecy.

Why would this intelligent, assertive, talented woman always do herself in at the point of stardom? What forces in her could be so great that even the most painful humiliation is unconsciously chosen over outstanding success?

We have to look into Dolly's history—as well as into her current psychological functioning—to explain her problem. Dolly's father fluctuated between being a millionaire and a pauper. But he always talked and acted as if he were a millionaire. Dolly's older brothers were superstars who achieved outstanding professional, economic, and social success, hobnobbing with famous people in the arts and politics. They treated her like a dopey kid sister, hardly ever allowing her in their world of glamour and grandeur. Dolly grew up like Cinderella, but always very close to the elite of the country. Like Cinderella, she had fantasies that her prince would come, that she too would enter this marvelous world. Her brothers, however, were not her princes, but more like the stepsisters who scoffed at Cinderella. Still, the contact she did have with her brothers and their friends brought her close to this much grandeur, enhancing her own fantasies of grandeur. She fantasized that some day she would be more rich and famous than her brothers, would be the superstar of the whole world, and would even put them to shame. In fact, she came pretty close to it in at least three or four fields. But, just as she reached the pinnacle, her fears of her own grandiosity became so overwhelming that she either produced a partial failure or left the milieu of her success.

Dolly had a fantasy about how it would feel to have done all the work before the exam. She experienced it as flying high up in the sky—and she became terrified, starting to shake and cry. Succeeding meant to her being God, or at least God-like. Gradually she began to admit—although very reluctantly—that she felt she was really much brighter, more talented, and more adept than any of her fellow students. Of course, in her secret little closet she really thought of herself as a true "Renaissance man"—like Leonardo da Vinci, with multiple talents in multiple fields. In fact, she did have extraordinary and diverse talents. But I had to remind her that she was not *really* in Leonardo's league. In her fantasy, she had surpassed him, but this fantasy frightened the daylights out of her. How could she be *that* grandiose? Once we had opened Pandora's box, a whole flood of fantasies poured out. She was not only the world's greatest speech therapist, but also the greatest singer, stage manager, wife, mother, cook, hostess. . . .

Once able to accept her fantasies with her keen sense of humor, she became much more life-sized in her view of herself—and so, incidentally, did her father, her mother, and her brothers. She had projected her grandiosity onto each of them, as well. She was on an ego trip merely by being a member of this "Royal Family." When she became conscious of all of this, she went through a period of real depression. What fun would life be without all this drama and grandeur, or the illusion of it? After a while, she realized that her *real* life was pretty satisfying and exciting, even without being dramatized. She was able both to study and actually to enjoy it. Passing or even getting a good mark on the test would not *really* make her surpass Leonardo—or perhaps her brothers.

Dolly is an excellent example of the vertical split. She did everything to attract admiration and applause, including the most direct thing—become a performer. But her achievements were completely split off from her, as was necessary because of her fear of her grandiosity. Once aware of it, she could drop her "fear of success" and enjoy her life-sized life.

Nora was a woman in her thirties who came into therapy for a variety of reasons. In one session she was trying to figure out why she was unable to utter a single word in the therapy group she attended. Nora was not a shy person; she was quite gracious and socially accomplished. She could handle a party or a group of strangers better than almost anyone, never feeling ill-at-ease in even the most cultured or intellectual social group. A therapy group is different, it is true. A patient in one would never be allowed to get away with putting up a social facade. But still, why this total inability to say a word?

In one of her private sessions, I asked Nora to say whatever came into her mind. She recalled her feelings in the group as being very similar to the feelings she had had all through school. Though she had been educated long before enforced busing, it happened that she was bused from her own middle-class WASP neighborhood to a school attended almost exclusively by lower-class, "shanty Irish" kids. Her mother came from a once wealthy family and always dressed Nora in an upper-class way. Nora was exposed to piano lessons, ballet lessons, poetry, literature, and cultivated manners. She stood out in her school like a sore thumb, attracting envy, and pure hatred from her underprivileged schoolmates. Nora's only defense was to keep her mouth shut. This continued through all her schooling—high school, college, and even graduate school. She never volunteered an answer, petrified she would be attacked and scorned by her peers.

What about this therapy group she was now attending? How did she feel about her social position there? At first, Nora denied feeling different from the rest of the group. Then, with much prodding, she began to admit reluctantly that she did feel she had more "class" than most of the other group members. She noted that she had gone out of her way to conceal from them her income, higher than that of some but not all of the group members. But the issue was not really an economic one. It was that—just as in grammar school —she felt she had a more socially prestigious position than any in the group, including myself. Though this was not necessarily so, Nora's fantasy was maintained by juggling the truth so that she could continue her covert and closeted feelings of grandiosity. Yes, Joe had a better education than she, but he was Jewish. Ruth was a WASP with a good social background, but she did not make as much money. I was ahead of her economically and educationally, and almost her equal culturally and socially, but I did not have quite the degree of *savoir-faire* that she possessed. Although a good argument could have been made for her feeling "superior" in each instance, the point was why was she involved in making these comparisons? And how did she always manage to come out on top in her thinking? Meanwhile, she was silent in group, and very modest and self-effacing in social meetings in the coffee shop after group. She was really so embarrassed about her grandiosity, and the fact that it might be discovered and attacked by the group as it had been in grammar school, that she had to remain totally hidden. She is a typical example of the horizontal split based on a fear of exposing grandiosity. When this was brought out of the closet, she was able to participate in group, and, along with this change, other changes began to occur in her life.

Judy was in one of my therapy groups. She began to talk about how nervous she was about an upcoming poetry reading, at which she was going to read some of her own work. She said the thought of this absolutely panicked her. I asked her to pretend it was the night of the reading and to get up in the group and recite one of her poems. She tried, but she said she felt as if she was paralyzed from the waist down; she could not get up from her chair. I asked her if she could recite one of her poems while she was seated. She began, but then said she could not continue—that she felt as if her mouth was full of mashed potatoes and she could utter only animal sounds. She became even more panicky at the thought of feeling like this on the night of the reading.

I asked her what she thought of her poetry. She said she was sure it was terrible. I asked her what she thought of us as an audience, or of her projected audience that night. She said she thought of us as monsters who were out to destroy her. Then I asked, if in a secret little part of her, she did not really think she had written a fantastically great poem—perhaps the greatest ever written—and that perhaps she had the fantasy of being the world's greatest creative genius. She blushed and smiled. Of course, she had had that *fantasy*, but she was sure it was not true—that her poem really was a terrible poem. I persisted. I said that, while I knew she *also* felt it was terrible, didn't she simultaneously think it was the greatest and that she was the world's greatest artistic genius? She smiled and stammered, but finally she admitted it. Then she was right, I said. I really would destroy her because I knew that *I* was the world's greatest genius. Another man in the group joined in the fun. He said he happened to know that we were both absolutely wrong because *he* was the world's greatest genius. At this point, the whole group was having a ball. We all joined in, letting her understand that grandiosity was not unique to her, that the rest of us would not destroy her for feeling it since we shared the feeling ourselves. Judy was laughing along with the rest of us.

I asked her to see if she could get up and recite one of her poems for us now. She hesitated, but with a little encouragement she rose and recited the poem in a beautiful, totally self-possessed way. We all told her the poem was lovely. She said she wanted to poll the group, allow every member to give her an opinion, so that she could take it in. They were truthful, sincere, and very complimentary. She could see they were not going to destroy her. And once she could admit her grandiose fantasies and laugh at them, her anxiety disappeared. But she also had to realize that her poem was neither the greatest nor the worst—just one of many very fine poems.

Judy, too, is an excellent example of a horizontal split. Her fear of her grandiosity, and of the attack it would bring on, tended to keep her silent and hidden. Once she could admit the grandiosity and bring herself down to life-size, she was able to seek admiration and take it in. Her poetry reading, which I attended, was quite a success.

Artists' blocks are frequently based, at least in part, on a fear promoted by grandiose fantasies. This is a fear of the artist both that he will lose control and become megalomaniac if he succeeds and a fear of the humiliation and mortification that he will experience if he fails—in other words, the horizontal split. Many artists have problems in this area. For one thing, they are exhibiting themselves—their acting, their singing, their writing, their painting. For another, there are no specific criteria in some fields for what *is* the greatest. Is this the greatest piece of non-fiction ever written? Of course. How can you prove otherwise? Suppose it doesn't sell? Well, that's because it's so far ahead of its time, people just don't understand its brilliance. It is even easier to view painting or composing this way. How many painters or composers, now world-famous, were thoroughly disparaged by the critics during their lifetime? And consider stage fright, so universal in the theater. At first, I was surprised to hear how world-famous entertainers suffered before each performance. But why not, if they haven't worked out their fears of grandiosity? For one thing, they have been exposed to more admiration and adulation than most other living persons. They have had fewer outside limits on their grandiosity than most. So they have compelling reasons for thinking that they are the greatest. And the higher they are, the farther they may fall. Suppose they fluff a line or turn in a poor performance. They will certainly be noticed by everyone, since all eyes will be riveted on them. Their humiliation will be tremendous and very public. Of all people, famous actors are likely to endure greater stage fright than an insignificant amateur in a local play.

I myself used to be absolutely panicked before I delivered a speech. I clung to my manuscript, my heart pounded like a sledgehammer, my knees knocked. I riveted my eyes on the paper as I read it and undoubtedly put everyone to sleep, even though what I had to say was of some interest. Now I don't experience significant anxiety when I speak in public or appear on television. I used to fantasize secretly that I would knock them dead, that I would be on "The Tonight Show" and make such a hit that I would replace Johnny Carson. Now I know that even if I am good, I will not be the greatest. I am not aiming at being the hero, so I am not so afraid that I will end up being the zero. My fears of humiliation diminished as I became aware of my grandiose fantasies.

CHAPTER 8

Grandiosity and Its Influence on Success

I have come upon an interesting problem among many of my analytic colleagues that, I believe, has its roots in grandiosity. Let me describe a typical example. Elise is a very successful practitioner of psychotherapy. She is extremely bright and she relates very well to people. She cares a great deal about her patients, and they perceive her conscientiousness, integrity, intelligence, and warmth. She rarely loses a patient and her patients refer other patients. Elise has had training in the basic discipline of psychology and psychotherapy, but she continues to take courses and supervision to enhance her professional growth. She has taken some classes with me and has been supervised by me. She is a very skilled, intuitive therapist, but she has read and currently reads practically nothing in her field. It happens that this field is changing almost daily. There are many important books and articles (such as Dr. Kohut's writings) that have profound effects on the diagnosis, conceptualization, and treatment of patients. To ignore the new material in our field is akin to a surgeon performing an appendectomy with a dull spoon. Now, Elise is so bright and so intuitive that she does a fairly good job anyway. But it is not nearly as good a job as she could do if she were familiar with the current literature. Of course, her patients do not know this. They know only that she is helping them, as, in truth, she is. They cannot possibly know how much more she could be helping them if she kept up with the literature.

But I, as her teacher and supervisor, know, and, more important, Elise knows. She tries to deny this, saying she is better than many therapists who have a great deal more knowledge of theory. She is probably right, because her natural gifts and her talents more than make up for her deficits. But when she is in class with her colleagues, Elise frequently feels terribly inferior and humiliated. Her classmates quote from books and articles she has never read and may even be unknown to her. She feels stupid, unworthy, guilty. Yet year after year goes by and still she does not read. What keeps her in this ridiculous, self-destructive pattern?

When I have analyzed this problem with Elise, and with many others in my field, invariably I have found that the answer lies in this issue of grandiosity. Down deep in some preconscious—but not totally unconscious—part of her, she feels that she is so intelligent, so intuitive that she can diagnose and treat a patient without needing to read what any of her more mortal colleagues have written. To stoop to this would be to admit that she is less than perfect. True, she takes classes and supervision as a balm to her conscience, in an attempt to fulfill her professional obligations, but she draws the line at reading.

Why does she draw the line here? Because if she read *and* took classes *and* was supervised, then how could she maintain her illusion of grandiosity in the face of having to acknowledge a professional error? This way she can say, "I'm the greatest. The reason I made the mistake was because I don't read. But if I did read, I would never make a mistake. I would be the greatest."

This dynamic is largely why people don't prepare adequately for tests or auditions, as well as the cause of the artist's block, in a more general sense. I have a patient for instance, who is a singer. She goes to auditions badly dressed, without practicing her song or even memorizing the lyrics. Invariably, she is turned down. But she can maintain her illusion that she is the world's greatest singer—that it was her lack of preparation that brought about her rejection. Suppose she was totally prepared, arrived on time, and looked her best—and still was rejected. She could nevertheless say that the world was not yet ready to appreciate her talent, though finding it a bit more difficult to maintain her grandiose illusions.

Artists are especially prone to these illusions. Greenwich Village is filled with authors who could write the great American novel, but somehow have never gotten around to it. If they have begun to write it, they have never quite finished it. If they have finished it, they have never sent it to a publisher. The same applies to painters or sculptors who never finish their works of art, or keep them hidden in closets if they do finish them. Did you know that Leonardo da Vinci never finished a painting? Freud wrote a monograph about him, and our current knowledge of narcissism would undoubtedly broaden our understanding of da Vinci and of this particular symptom of his.

You do not have to be a great artist or therapist to have this problem. How often have you allowed for the possiblity of failure by not really trying your best to succeed? Some of the time, there may be other factors involved, to be sure, but the maintenance of the illusion of grandiosity may be a major issue for many of you. If you really tried your very best and still didn't get that promotion, it would be a lot more difficult for you to continue to believe that *you* were really the best of the lot, that *you* deserved the promotion. This way, you tell yourself that you don't really care whether you got it or not. Joe got it because he is a "yes man" and "sucks up" to the boss. You can go on feeling that you are much more talented than Joe, that he got it because he pushed for it and you didn't. Actually, you may be right. You may have lost the job because you were afraid to put your self-esteem on the line by going all out to try to get it.

We ordinary human beings have enough problems about our grandiosity. These problems usually revolve around our fear of loss of control of our grandiosity and our fear of humiliation, which make us put dampers on our self-esteem. But what about famous people—especially those who, in reality, have almost no limits at all on their power? Their problems over grandiosity are often of a very different nature. If they are absolute dictators or in positions of nearly unlimited power, humiliation or scorn is frequently not a realistic possibility for them. Their problems revolve around the lack of outside limits (or at least enough) on their grandiosity. Their grandiosity can be allowed a full expression, and, unless they have very powerful internal limits, they can cause their subjects, their countries, and sometimes themselves almost inconceivable difficulties.

Recently I was discussing the atrocities in Uganda under the rule of Idi Amin. Amin, if you recall, had six bearers carry him into a meeting while he was seated on a platform. That was only a mild form of his grandiosity. Apparently he has a large harem of women. If a minor utterance of one of his subjects—or even of a foreigner—in Uganda displeases him, he orders this person to be executed. He is the total dictator, there is no check on any of his whims. In my conversation about Amin, my friend said, "You know, there are rumors that he's had brain damage from tertiary syphilis. He is mad and therefore not responsible for his actions."

I smiled, recalling to him that the same rumors had circulated about Mussolini, Hitler, some of the Spanish conquistadores, and many others with a great deal of power which they'd misused. I think we have an aversion to the idea that anyone except a madman or a brain-damaged leader could perpetrate such atrocities. We do not like to think that the mere possession of this kind of power is apt to affect someone more like ourselves—*not* mad and *not* brain-damaged—in this horrifying manner. I cannot prove that the people I have cited, or many others—Nixon, J. Edgar Hoover, Napoleon, Marie Antoinette, to name a few—did not suffer brain damage or were not mad. However, I feel that the reason we prefer to think this about them is that we are horrified by the prospect of what we—ordinary people—might do if we possessed this kind of power. It is our fear of the poor controls on our own grandiosity that makes us want to view *them* as the victims of some strange, exotic illness. Too many with unlimited power over others—victors and vanquished, masters and slaves, teachers and students—have misused their power greatly and destructively.

I do not think Amin is "sick," nor were Hitler and Mussolini. I think their excesses were functions of their grandiosity, which had free rein without any checks. Our constitution very wisely set up an all but infallible system of checks and balances. Yet, even in our country, there have been flagrant examples of the abuses that derive from the possession of power.

Lawrence of Arabia is another dramatic example of a man of apparent genius who had all sorts of troubles dealing with his grandiosity. He was so overwhelmed by his success that he enlisted as a simple soldier in the British Army in order to attain an anonymity that might counter his grandiosity. From early in his childhood, he felt he was destined for greatness. At the same time, he struggled to purge his heroic fantasies from his mind by becoming an unknown laborer. He flirted with death constantly—almost testing his mortality in a counterphobic way by driving motorcycles at inordinately high speeds, which, indeed, finally led to his death in an accident.

Kipling wrote a poem entitled "If I Were King." What would you do if you were king or queen and had absolute, unlimited power. Would you be a benevolent ruler? Perhaps. But Caligula was not and Henry VIII was not and Indira Gandhi was not. Most of us thought Madame Gandhi would use her power to improve the lot of her countrymen. Remember what happened. Most Americans considered J. Edgar Hoover a pillar of virtue and justice. Nixon was elected by one of the largest electoral votes in American history. Most Americans must have regarded him as a dedicated, selfless, honest public servant. The "arrogance of power" is a newly coined phrase in America, but it has been anything but new in the history of the world. Are you sure you could keep your grandiosity in check, and be a just and kind ruler, if you were an absolute dictator? I hope so, but frankly I would not bet on it. So, you see, some of our fears of our grandiosity may not be so irrational after all. Apparently it is human nature to become very grandiose with no outside checks. However, since *we* are not dictators, except perhaps in very limited spheres, the degree of our fear is usually disproportionate, since we do not have the possibility of going "mad" with our power.

But history gives credence to these fears of loss of control and the incredible excesses that follow. History also gives us many examples of people whose lack of control of their grandiosity resulted in their humiliation, disgrace, and even death. In recent years, there were Nixon, Mitchell, Haldeman, Erlichman, and many others in the executive branch of our government. Many of us were alive during both the excesses and the destruction of Hitler and Mussolini. Nazi war criminals have been—and are still being—brought to justice. The prime minister of Israel was forced to resign because of indiscretions. Madame Gandhi was defeated at the polls. And during the French Revolution, two hundred years ago, Marie Antoinette was beheaded. The loss of control that leads to excesses is not infrequently followed by shame, humiliation, or worse. Our fears of toppling from the pinnacle of power into the mud *do* have a basis in fact and in history. Even though our fears for ourselves may be greatly exaggerated, they are not totally inappropriate. We do need to maintain a certain control on our grandiosity, but only if there are no strong, effective external controls. For almost all of us there are plenty, if not too many, so we do not have to defend ourselves by putting such restraint over our self-esteem. We have no need for a horizontal split that stifles our positive feelings about ourselves, or a vertical split that disowns the person who is getting the praise, that pushes the compliments away from ourselves.

CHAPTER 9

Admit Your Grandiose Fantasies

Hopefully, you can see now that many of our problems with self-esteem arise from our fears of our grandiose fantasies. We are afraid of our grandiosity because we are not sure we can control it once we let it out of the closet. We are afraid of becoming so vain and megalomaniacal that we will be totally obnoxious, rejected by our friends and loved ones. We are also afraid that, like that omnipotent baby ruler, we may become vicious, destructive tyrants, totally lacking in sympathy for anyone who happens to thwart our wishes. Our conscience and our moral system would find that state of affairs totally unacceptable. Even if somehow we got past those barriers, in the end we might be punished, even killed, for our tyranny. But, in some ways, worse even than the fear of being killed is the fear of humiliation and mortification.

Others might ridicule us for thinking we were somebody special, when in fact they see us as being quite ordinary. Imagine how it would feel to hear people say, "Look who thinks he's good-looking." Or, "She thinks she's smart—that dumb-dumb." Or, "She feels she's sensitive; she's got about as much sensitivity as a brick wall." The humiliation of considering yourself somebody special and having your vision shot down and laughed at is a possibility most of us would find absolutely unbearable.

So what do we do? To avoid the risk of being a hero—of becoming so vain or destructive that we face the specter of humiliation—we prefer to play it safe by being a zero. This avoids all the dangers, but what a price to pay! We have to go through life minimizing our joy, our pleasure, our success, just so we won't get too uppity. We have to play ourselves down, be shy, self-effacing, and humble (the horizontal split). Others among us must go through life constantly pushing ourselves to attract attention, applause, and recognition. Even after we acquire what we seek so compulsively, we aren't able to take any of it in (the vertical split). Either way, of course, our self-esteem has to be kept low, subdued, never allowed to soar too high or for too long for fear it will come crashing down.

This is a pretty sad state of affairs. What can we do about it? The examples you read of my patients with this problem all pointed in the same direction. The way they were able to release their good feelings about themselves and allow themselves to perform more effectively—to take in the praise that they sought and deserved—was their admission of their grandiose fantasies. Remember, none of these people really knew they had these fantasies. They would have said, and in fact did say, as I am sure *you* will, "But that isn't me. That might be Muhammad Ali or his pal, Howard Cosell. They obviously think they're the greatest. But that certainly isn't me."

Let us have a little dialogue.

R: "I know it isn't you *on the surface*. That's what I've been telling you. I know that you feel lacking in confidence and not very smart or attractive or effective."

Y: "So why are you telling me I feel the opposite? That I really think I'm the greatest? That's a lot of baloney."

R: "Mister, you're not listening. You're not hearing me right. I didn't say you thought you were the greatest. What I am saying is that somewhere in you, almost but not quite completely out of your awareness, hidden in a closet that you keep locked, are some fantasies of being much greater than you really *know*, in your head, that you are."

Y: "That's ridiculous. You're talking just like a psychoanalyst! There's some part of me that I don't really even know about that's completely screwing me up. Baloney!"

R: "That's what I'm saying. But I'm also saying that that part of you isn't as inaccessible to you as you think it is. It wasn't inaccessible for my patients and it wasn't for me."

Y: "OK. How do I find out about it? With an X ray or an electroencephalogram or a Rorschach test? Or do you want me to spend thousands of dollars getting analyzed like you or your patients? I don't have that kind of time or money, and I'm not sure I'd want to spend it that way even if I did have it."

R: "I agree. I'm not asking you to do any of those things. I just want you to try to follow me and to answer a few questions truthfully."

Y: "OK."

R: "First of all, I want to make clear to you the difference between a thought and a fantasy. I don't *think* I'm the smartest guy in the world, but sometimes I *feel* that I am. I don't *think* I can beat Jimmy Connors at tennis, but sometimes I fantasize that I could. So what I'm asking you about is not your intellectual evaluation of yourself but your fantasy, get it?"

Y: "Yeah, OK."

R: "Now, haven't you, at some time, fantasized that you could write a best-selling novel, that your own life and experiences would be so interesting that if you could get them down on paper, you could win a Nobel Prize?"

Y: "No, not really. I do feel my life is pretty interesting, but I know I can't write. So I've never had that fantasy."

R: "What sport do you play?"

Y: "Nothing much except touch football in the park on Sunday."

R: "Well, have you ever had the fantasy that, if you had really worked at it, you could have been a better quarterback than Joe Namath? Ever felt that you could call the plays better than Namath or his coach?"

Y: "Well, yes, sometimes when I'm out there on Sundays and I throw a beautiful, long pass for a touchdown, I do dream that I could be doing it at the Super Bowl."

R: "Well, that's what I mean. And tell me, don't you fantasize that you are really the world's greatest lover—that no one else is so sensitive to exactly what a woman needs?"

Y: "Well, I guess I do sometimes, but I also worry about whether I'll be able to have an erection the next time I make love."

R: "But those two things are not at all incompatible. You're either a hero or a zero, omnipotent or literally impotent."

Y: "Oh, I see. And all I have to do is to get in touch with and admit whatever grandiose fantasies I have been hiding. Like, sometimes, I feel I really understand more about what life is all about than all of you analysts put together."

R: "*That* part may not even be a fantasy. Oh no, now *I'm* being self-effacing. Yes, yes. That's exactly what I'm saying you have to begin to admit to yourself."

Y: "So what if I admit it? Big deal. What's so important about admitting it? You're right. I fool around painting landscapes. Sometimes I have the fantasy that I could be better than Constable or Turner or any of them, if I really kept at it."

R: "Well, if you take that out of the closet and expose it to the light of day, it's no longer going to be so scary that you have to keep your self-esteem down to protect yourself. It's just like my patient who fantasized she was the world's greatest creative genius. Once she could expose that, she could laugh at it. She could see she wasn't the world's greatest creative genius, because *I* am."

Y: "No, *I* am. Now I'm beginning to get it. Once you let it out of hiding, you can laugh at it because it's so absurd. But you don't have to feel humiliated either, because you can use your sense of humor to cope with it."

R: "Right. Now I want you really to try to unlock the closet. Do you remember James Thurber's Walter Mitty? Danny Kaye was in a movie about him, called *The Secret Life of Walter Mitty*. It was probably before your time, but you may have seen it on television. Walter Mitty was a meek little guy who had all these fantasies of being a great military hero, detective, lover, and a lot of other kinds of superstars."

Y: "That was before my time, but I get the idea."

R: "Then, more recently, Woody Allen was in a picture called *Play It Again, Sam*. Again, here is a meek little guy, a total loser with women, who had a fantasy of being Humphrey Bogart. The picture ends with him doing that great scene from *Casablanca*."

Y: "Oh, yeah, I remember that one."

R: "As a matter of fact, *I* just remembered I really used to fantasize that *I* was Humphrey Bogart. Have you ever fantasized being Bogart, or pitching in the World Series, or being a sultan with a harem, or getting to be the president of your company?"

Y: "Yes, I guess I have. I plead guilty."

R: "Well, there's nothing to feel guilty or even ashamed about. Almost all of us have those fantasies at some time. It is not strange or abnormal to have them, but most of us feel that it is. And we get up these elaborate defenses against even admitting them to ourselves. One of the things that will really help you with your self-esteem is to admit the fantasies and to keep on acknowledging them openly, with a sense of humor, every time one of them whisks through your mind. Don't let them shoot through so fast you don't even recognize that they're there."

Y: "And just doing that will have such a tremendous effect on my self-esteem? That's hard to believe."

R: "I agree. That *is* hard to believe. It took me more than twenty-five years as an analyst, constantly scrutinizing my own and other people's feelings, to find out about it. And then I was able to understand it mainly through these books I read. But believe me, it *is* true. And it *does* work. I've given you several examples of people for whom it has worked, and I could give you many more. Just try it and see."

CHAPTER 10

Grandiosity and God

Before we leave the subject of grandiosity, I would like to try to explain the reason I think that people believe in God. The vast majority of the people in the world believe in some kind of deity. Though there is hardly any "scientific" proof of the existence of a deity, even careful scientists, who would subject any other of their beliefs to the most exacting scrutiny, can maintain a steadfast believe in God without one iota of such proof. What is it that makes a belief in God so universal? And, further, why is it we are so sure that *our* particular God is the real one, and all others are merely idols worshiped by savages or unsophisticated, mistaken people? How is it that I feel a certain amount of discomfort even in writing this chapter, feeling I will offend readers who may believe that even searching for some explanation of faith in God constitutes a kind of heresy or blasphemy?

Nevertheless, despite these hesitations, I must proceed. If you can accept the whole premise of an unconscious or preconscious grandiose part of yourself—and also of your tremendous fear of it and your need to repress it—then it seems to me the explanation for belief in God becomes rather self-evident. We keep hidden away this all-knowing, all-powerful part of ourselves, and whenever it intrudes on our consciousness, we are frightened that it will break out of control, frightened that *we* may become egomaniacal, destructive, and self-destructive tyrants like Idi Amin. Or else we are afraid of being subjected to humiliation if this part of us should begin to show. Maintaining our defenses against this part of ourselves makes us minimize our joy and exhilaration, and diminishes our effectiveness and our self-esteem. Defending ourselves against the part of us that feels perfect also prevents our seeking out or taking in appropriately deserved compliments and admiration. Projecting our own hidden grandiosity onto our parents or mates or children or friends causes us terrible errors in judgment and brings about all kinds of difficulties in our intimate relationships. So what can we do to avoid or help solve these problems?

One thing we can do is to create a figure outside of ourselves, outside of anyone we happen to know, and project all of our feelings of our own grandeur and perfection onto him. By creating a God, we disown our own feelings of omnipotence. It is not we who are vain about our perfection, omnipotence, and omniscience. The figure of God has become the repository of all these personally unacceptable feelings. The mortal person will not be punished for his vanity or die from his self-centeredness, as did Narcissus. He has a figure outside of himself, a figure he never sees or has to deal with in the real world, a figure he is free to worship and adore as he could never allow himself to worship and adore himself. Think of the qualities we attribute to our God. He is all-powerful, all-knowing, infallible, perfect, beautiful, loving, compassionate, forgiving, the creator of heaven and earth. He is pretty close, in fact, to being what an omnipotent baby must feel he is.

In my opinion, the reason for the universality of the belief in God is that it appears to be a perfect solution to man's problems of dealing with his grandiosity. Man not only projects his grandiosity, but he can disown it, and can continue to give and get adoration without realizing that it is a part of himself that is the recipient of it. He does not have to deal with his fear of losing control of his grandiosity because he has put it *outside* of himself. He does not have to deal with a real person who might use this omnipotent power against him.

I think that the reason for acceptance of and worship of rulers has many of the same roots as belief in God. It is difficult, otherwise, to explain why a democratic and sophisticated people like the British still has a queen. The degree of worship accorded the Japanese emperor, some conquerors by conquered people, and even our own president is difficult to explain without taking grandiosity into account. But a belief in God appears to be the perfect solution to handling the problem of grandiosity. And, of course, by accepting this solution we have the backing of society and, frequently, also of the important figures around us, such as our parents. Being religious, in almost all of the world (with the recent exceptions of Russia and China), is equated with being virtuous.

Is there any fly in the ointment? Is there any price we pay for projecting our grandiosity outside of ourselves and onto God? I think there is. First of all, this transaction depends on a dismissal of some of our reality testing and on a continued belief in primitive magical thinking. We must suspend our scientific judgment and have faith in a system without proof. We remain superstitious. For instance, are you superstitious? If you are, it means, for one thing, that you are not dealing squarely with reality, which is bound to interfere with your using your best judgment. Secondly, in creating this force outside of yourself, you must, to some extent, give up your sense of your autonomy, your independence, and your belief in your own responsibility for what happens in your life. The suspension of this responsibility can often bring about a failure in the ability to make your own decisions. Besides, almost any religious system contains dogma associated with the mystical aspect of the religion. The necessity of following the dogma—the rules and regulations—in order to stay in God's good graces, can severely limit your freedom to make autonomous choices that might enrich your experience and your adventure in life. One clear example of this can be found in the sexual restrictions that invariably seem to accompany any religious system. Sex is just one area in which you give up your freedom and autonomy by following another's rules—not your own.

It is a well-known fact that one cannot get anywhere in an argument about religion. I am not trying to convert true believers. Nor do I presume to know all ultimate answers to ultimate religious queries. But if you have followed the argument about grandiosity thus far, you will probably be able to see a connection between this thesis and an explanation of the universality of the belief in God. More intellectual believers, who are apt to see God in a symbolic rather than in a real sense, might observe that the discussion thus far even supported their belief. They might feel that for most human beings, gains in dealing with their problems about grandiosity by a strong belief in a real and personal deity might far outweigh the loss in reality-testing and autonomy. That is a personal choice which you, the reader, will have to make. But to make it freely, it helps to understand all the dimensions involved.

CHAPTER 11

Narcissistic Extensions: Raising Your Self-esteem Through Connections with Others

How do we make up for the real or imagined lacks that our self-images reflect? Some of us feel unattractive, others socially inept, others not very bright. One way we try to deal with these real or imagined limitations is to attach ourselves to people whom we feel will make up for the deficit our self reveals to us. Let us remember that the deficit is not necessarily an objectively real one; it is not necessarily in our *selves*, but in our *self-images*. It is subjective, rather than objective.

How often have you seen a brainy, wealthy, but rather unattractive little man with a tall, not very bright, beautiful woman on his arm? This may be a perfect example of two people choosing their mates because of what is called a *narcissistic extension*. Let us say that the man feels unattractive physically. He may also *be* unattractive in reality. Our subjective view of ourselves may certainly be affected by reality. Hopefully, there would be some correlation between one's self-image and reality. The healthier we are, the better our reality-testing. Let us say that this man who is, in fact, unattractive, also *feels* unattractive. As we have said before, there are some unattractive people who feel attractive and some attractive people who feel unattractive. In the case of our particular small man with the tall woman, his self-image—as far as his physical appearance goes—is in keeping with reality. He tries to make up for what he perceives as a deficit in his looks by attaching himself to a beautiful woman, and, feeling self-conscious about being short, he picks a tall woman to make up for that deficit in his self-image as well. Now let us imagine that the woman on his arm correctly views herself as being beautiful. However, she doesn't feel very bright, capable, or effective. The man she has picked is intelligent and successful, so she has tried to make up for a deficit in herself by attaching herself to a man who possesses the qualities she feels she lacks. Actually, her image of herself may also be consonant with reality; perhaps she is not very bright, has not accomplished very much. Henry Kissinger, when a bachelor, was reputed by the press to have outstanding success with women, despite a rather dull personality and not very good looks. Reporters asked him what it was he had that made him so successful with women. "Power," he is supposed to have answered. And then there is the old joke about the men's cologne that is supposed to be a tremendous aphrodisiac for women; it smells like money.

Despite the fact that these anecdotes may sound somewhat sexist, in our present society, as in other societies past and present, the man with power has attracted the woman with looks. This is a simplistic example of trying to deal with lacks in one's self-image by narcissistic extension. Others might be subtler, such as a shy, modest, self-effacing man picking a charismatic, exhibitionistic woman.

As a matter of fact, men in our society have a rather difficult time expressing their physical exhibitionism in any direct manner. Men's fashions have become more flamboyant lately, but still men are not encouraged to exhibit themselves as women are. One very interesting way by which men deal with social taboos on male physical exhibitionism is the amount of attention they pay to magazines like *Playboy* and the degree of girl-watching that goes on. Women, though they too look at attractive men, are not nearly as involved as men are with voyeurism. The sexual perversion of voyeurism— or peeping—in men has no counterpart in women. Women are certainly allowed much more expression in physical exhibitionism both in dress and undress. I think men unconsciously envy the woman's ability to display herself for admiration. Perhaps one of the unconscious reasons men are drawn to *Playboy*—and to burlesque, strip shows, and the Folies Bergère—is because they can get a vicarious release for their own closet exhibitionism by identifying with the naked woman who is displaying herself. I do not mean to imply that this is the only psychodynamic involved, but I believe it is a very important one.

I had a patient who was tremendously drawn to all kinds of voyeuristic activity, and who was very modest and self-effacing. As he began to be able to seek out attention and admiration in appropriate ways, his interest in peeping diminished markedly. There may have been other factors that I missed, but I was really impressed with the change in him. Incidentally, by no means am I trying to say that voyeuristic activity is bad, immoral, or neurotic. I feel that people should do whatever turns them on, if it causes no one else any harm. The male habit of finding vicarious expression for exhibitionism and need for admiration by girl-watching seems perfectly appropriate to me. I think it is an example of getting admiration through a specific and interesting kind of narcissistic extension.

Women, on the other hand—though allowed physical exhibition through clothing and such display—have been permitted very little expression of their intellectual, creative, and artistic potential. Unfortunately, until the past twenty years and often still today, many women live in the shadow of their husbands' professional, intellectual, or artistic successes. Many of them do little to realize their own considerable talents, using husbands as narcissistic extensions for their thwarted need for admiration in these areas.

Mates are not the only people we can use as extensions. "Child-wearing" may be a familiar term to many. We all know about the woman who is constantly referring to "my son, the doctor." Many parents, either self-effacing or frustrated in realizing their own potential, place upon their children the burden of performing for them. Often they then secretly take the credit for having produced the doctor, or the superstar athlete, or the famous actress. Children quickly pick up the way to please us. In many instances, they go in the direction that *we* want them to go, to achieve recognition for *us*, rather than in the direction that is motivated by their own personality. I have known many people who became accomplished musicians, artists, or professionals in order to live out their parents' dreams and fantasies. Several, having achieved those goals, just as quickly dropped them; the success was not really theirs but their parents', or one parent's vicarious means of enhancing his or her self-love. In a way, I did this myself. I became a doctor to please my father, but then spoiled it all for him by becoming a psychiatrist. I tell parents to be very cautious about pushing their children too hard academically, in sports, or artistically. If Johnny keeps forgetting to practice the piano and runs off to play baseball, maybe you'd better wonder for whom those piano lessons really are—Johnny or you.

The reason we are so prone to project onto someone else our own need for approval and attention lies in our strong taboos against expressing these needs more directly. Much of the time, these vicarious ways of finding approval do not work out very well. If we pick a mate because of some particular quality or charisma that we lack, we may derive a certain amount of satisfaction from this for a while. But almost invariably what finally develops is an envy and a hostility toward the mate for being able to get so easily what always eludes us. Eventually, instead of enjoying the reflected glory as a way of indirectly getting something for ourselves, we may come to feel even more erased and negated by the constant direction of attention away from us. Marriages that are based on an unspoken contract

of enhancing self-images through narcissistic extension
have a poor long-term outlook, as I will illustrate—especially from examples of psychotherapists themselves
and their marital problems.

In the long run, "child-wearing" is also usually a
destructive and self-destructive procedure. At some
point, the children begin to resent being used to satisfy
the parents' needs, and often they "get" the parents
where it hurts the most—by failing in the plan that was
charted by the parents' own need for admiration
through extension. Incidentally, mates and children are
not the only targets of narcissistic extension. People often choose their friends on the basis of some quality
that is lacking in their own self-image. The "nouveau-
riche" social climber, who feels socially inadequate and
inferior, may pick his friends because of social position
only. I have a patient who came from very humble
origins. Her father was a member of a degraded minor-
ity group. Her mother pretended to be a WASP
(White Anglo-Saxon Protestant) and was fairly well-
educated, though a slovenly housekeeper and very
neglectful of her daughter. The patient lived on the
fringe of an area housing many upper-class families;
her schoolmates were often quite wealthy. She suffered
many humiliations in school because she was poorly
dressed, dirty, had head lice, and was obviously from
the wrong side of the tracks. She made up her mind at
an early age that she would reverse these childhood
humiliations, that she would penetrate the upper crust
of New York society, no matter what it took her to get
there. She has achieved her end, but at terrible cost.
She has had several husbands, all of them wealthy and
socially prominent. She has arrived in the highest
circles of society, but her husbands have been terrible
people—alcoholics, dope addicts, wife beaters. In her
attempt to enhance her social self-image, she has
neglected to seek out the qualities in a mate that would
have made her happy.

Let us examine the stories of others whose choice of
partners is much too influenced by their need for nar-

cissistic extensions, and let us consider some of the difficulties this may cause.

Dick and Harry are two men in their forties who have had difficulty with women throughout their lives. Dick falls in love with every woman he meets. He likes to kid about how he proposes on the first date. He hasn't *really* done that, but he's come pretty close. He's been married four times and would have had two or three other wives, except that the women luckily—for him and for them—turned him down.

Harry has never been able to find a woman who really interests him. After a date or two or three, he loses whatever drive he has had toward a woman and moves on to another, only to have the same thing happen again.

June is in her thirties. She will go out with or marry only extraordinarily handsome men. Unfortunately, being handsome is not one of the important requirements of a good husband or even a good lover.

They sound pretty different, don't they? Yet they all have basic problems in the same area of their psyche—their self-image. None has a high regard for himself. This doesn't necessarily reveal itself to an observer, though none of them is especially confident or happy despite the outer signs of worldly success. All are respected professionals—bright, conscientious, and respected by their peers. All have achieved many of what most think are the ingredients of a "good life," but none of them is happy or satisfied, and none really likes himself.

Dick's number is this. He doesn't really think much of himself, so he projects onto every woman he meets the idea of the perfect person he himself would like to be. He idealizes her. Whatever she really is, he thinks she is the most wonderful, beautiful, intelligent, warm, loving person he himself would like to be. He then proceeds to "fall in love" with this ideal, rather than with the reality of who the woman is.

Have you ever done this? Actually, it isn't particularly unique. "Falling in love" almost always has for all of us some elements of the quality of idealization. "Falling in love" has been described by many psychiatrists as a "normal psychosis." People tend to lose their reality-testing ability when they "fall in love." They almost always tend to idealize the other person—to project their grandiosity on to them. Strangely enough, they also see all kinds of similarities between themselves and the other person. "We have so much in common." The person they are really "in love" with is a projection of an idealized part of themselves. They cannot openly acknowledge their own fantasy of grandiosity, so they attach it to someone else and then proceed to love it in this other person.

Dick carries this common "normal" experience to an extreme degree. He is totally convinced of the perfection, the flawlessness of the woman he invests with such qualities. Perhaps some of you female readers have been on the receiving end of this process. Despite the fact that, in someone like Dick, you have an admirer constantly telling you that he loves you, reacting to you as if you were the greatest thing since television, there is something hollow, something empty about his words. As much as you like to receive praise, there is something about *this* kind of praise that isn't very nourishing. Actually, it doesn't nourish because it isn't really directed toward you. Rather, it is a projection of someone else's *idea* of you. And it may have very little indeed to do with who you really are.

Back to Dick and his number. He has now projected this marvelous ideal onto some poor, unsuspecting woman. Dick is very intelligent, charming, and attractive. He has such a winning way with words that, at first, the woman may buy—or at least want to buy— the picture of herself that she gets from him. Besides, Dick is quite a good catch, so many women are drawn to him. Since he is rich, has status, and what he is proposing is marriage—not uncommitted sex or orgies or a housekeeping arrangement—many women certainly see him as sincere and desirable. And, after all, he is *not* Tommy Manville; his marriages have lasted a mini-

mum of five years. Many women are willing to overlook his track record as bad luck or bad judgment.
Dick's marriages do last a while because his disillusion-
ment (and this word is used in its specific sense) may
not occur for several years. But once it occurs—and, of
course, it is bound to—and Dick sees that his wife is
just another mortal, not the ideal he has projected onto
her, he loses interest and begins to look for his next
"victim." Of course, he finds her, and so the story re-
peats itself.

As I have said, Dick's problem is that he does not,
and cannot, feel that he himself is a prize—a fine,
worthwhile, attractive man. He cannot think of himself
in realistically positive terms, so he must make up for
this by projecting an idealized, grandiose image onto
his partner. That way—by associating himself with
her—through a narcissistic extension, vicariously (and
temporarily) he gets a boost in his self-esteem.

Let's take poor Harry next. At least Dick's life is full
of (temporary) love and (illusory) romance. Harry's is
a desert. His problem is also his self-esteem, but in
practice it works out quite differently from Dick's. He
goes out with a girl; very quickly he decides she is not
good enough for him to pursue. He, too, is looking for
an idealized partner, but *he is unable to project it.* His
standard of perfection is *so* high that *no* one can ever
begin to reach it; all women are excluded by him. Like
Dick, he does not really think well of himself, not with
any consistency. He too needs to project an idealized
image. He thinks so little of himself that he needs an
absolutely perfect woman to make up for this deficit in
his self-esteem. But he is more realistic than Dick. He
sees the reality of the women he meets and he can
never be satisfied with any of them. Harry, like Dick, is
trying to express his grandiosity through projecting it,
but he is unable to do so. Since the basic reason for his
attachment to a woman is to project his grandiosity, to
make her into a narcissistic extension rather than to
fulfill his realistic needs for closeness, he can never find
a mate.

June is a reasonably attractive woman in her thirties. She has been a very successful professional and makes more money than 99 percent of the women in America. But June is hooked on handsome men. There is nothing wrong with a woman preferring handsome men, but June is so obsessed with male physical appearance that she overlooks the person inside. So June has had a succession of very handsome husbands and lovers, who have been absolutely terrible for her as people. Some haven't nearly approached her talent or intelligence, and bored her. Some have been out-and-out scoundrels, and hurt her. What is this preoccupation June has with physical appearance? Well, even though most of us would find June quite attractive, her image of herself is that of an ugly woman, disgustingly ugly.

June has a very vain and very competitive mother, plus an older sister who was a beauty queen. June's mother consistently disparaged June's physical appearance, telling June that her breasts were too small and her thighs were too big, that her nose was crooked and that she was overweight. June was conditioned to think of herself as the ugly duckling. Comparison with a sister who was a Homecoming Queen at college, and who was seen by her mother as an extension of her own beauty, compounded the situation. So June's physical self-image was very poor. Again we must distinguish between the objective reality of June, who is a relatively attractive woman, and her own subjective reality or her self-image, that of an unattractive woman.

So June needs an especially beautiful man to enhance her own low physical self-image, though such a man may not make a particularly effective mate.

Lay people are not alone in having problems in relating to others because of self-image. It is well-known that psychotherapists also have trouble in their most intimate relationships. They seem to have a great deal of difficulty in relating to their mates, and this difficulty follows a particular pattern. In general, therapists seem to be drawn to mates who are less secure, less mature than they are. Therapists are looking for those who will admire them, for mates to whom *they* will be narcissistic extensions, and to whom they can be helpful and supportive. Yet, instead of nourishing confidence, this support tends to sabotage the growth and development of the therapist's mate, often reducing him or her to the status of another patient on the schedule. The therapist ultimately feels deprived of having his own needs for support met. Serious difficulties result which often bring about divorce.

This disease of psychotherapists seems to cut across all lines—sex lines, sexual-preference lines, generational lines, and ethnic lines. I am fairly sure that the pathogenic agent is the tendency we therapists have toward feeling grandiose. After all, we are often deified by our patients. To put it simply, or simplistically, therapists' intimate, personal relationships appear to be an extension, almost a perversion of their work. They tend to be drawn to partners who have rather serious emotional problems and who are looking for a wise, understanding person to help, support, and perhaps "cure" them. The therapists are motivated by their own feelings of grandiosity and omnipotence. They think they will be able—by love, care and wisdom—to make this person happy, especially one who has frustrated several previous therapists' efforts to accomplish this.

Of course, the therapists feel very noble and generous in this endeavor, but their satisfactions are hardly altruistic alone. They start by getting tremendous adulation and admiration from their "sick" mates, who usually make them into narcissistic extensions. Beginning the relationship in an unchallenged position of superiority and control, they are always "right" or "healthy," their mate is always "wrong" or "sick." Besides gratifying their need to be admired, this balance also gives a perfect assurance of acceptance by their mates, and a near guarantee against being abandoned.

Most therapists' self-image, other than in their professional role, usually leaves a good deal to be desired.

In contrast to the generally accepted view that therapists are models of mental health, quite the reverse is true. That old chestnut, "You don't have to be crazy to be a psychiatrist, but it helps," contains a great deal of truth. Most people who enter the field become interested in it as a means of trying to understand and deal with tensions that they feel within themselves. In many ways, the experience of a variety of emotional problems helps them understand and be able to empathize with their patients. Now, hopefully, by means of the intensive, long-lasting analysis that all qualified psychoanalysts must undergo—and many other therapists choose to—some of their own problems will have been resolved.

But we analysts know that getting treatment in dealing with a problem is hardly the same as not having the problem at all. Some of the most famous psychoanalysts—Fritz Perls, Sandor Rado, J. L. Moreno, to name a few—are among the most insecure men I have ever met. Even Freud was hardly a model of mental health. By his own admission, he worried constantly about his professional status and was concerned that his patients might leave him. Freud recommended that analysts have frequent reanalyses throughout their career to deal with issues unresolved by earlier treatment.

Since it was often their personal insecurities and faltering self-images that led therapists into the field in the first place, many, or even most of them, retain these insecurities about themselves as people. By continuing a quasi-professional role in their intimate relationships, they are presenting a part of themselves —their professional self—that most feel the most secure about.

At the outset, the therapist's match seems to have been made in heaven. In truth, there is often a period of especial bliss, apparently perfect fulfillment, for both partners. The mate has finally found his or her savior, the perfect projection for the individual's grandiosity. He or she has found someone who is deeply interested

in him as a person—interested in his childhood, his
past, his troubles. He has found a sympathetic, understanding, loving mate who appears to cherish him, who
wants to help him grow as a person. He has found
someone on whom he can lean when necessary; he can
expose all his weakness and invariably get a warm, caring response. At last he can relax and feel totally cared
for in an emotional sense. The dream of finding a perfect parent, or God, has come true. This parent has the
additional advantage of being a certified expert in
parenting. What better person to put in charge of one's
self? After all, others, his patients, are relying on this
savior-mate all week long. He really does listen; he has
been trained to do so. He is wiser, more sensitive, more
perceptive than most, and he can always come up with
a theoretical explanation for every anxiety, every depression, every psychosomatic symptom. Who could
ask for a more perfect mate? Besides, most therapists
are hard workers and good providers, and it doesn't
hurt to have someone taking good care of you in this
way, too. In addition, the therapist has a good public
image. He or she is an especially good catch—a perfect
narcissistic extension. One of my female patients had a
fantasy of having as a harem a group of psychiatric
residents at Mt. Sinai Hospital. That would have to be
the absolute zenith of many young women's dreams.
So, indeed, it is a union made in heaven for the
mate—at least, at the outset.

What about the therapist? Here, too, the beginning
provides what seems to be unmitigated bliss. Finally
the therapist has found a person who truly admires
him—who gratifies his grandiose needs for adoration—a person who trusts him, respects him, looks
up to him as a special sage, as his own mother probably did not. His patients may feel that way about him
at times, but he takes a great deal of hostility from
them in addition to the admiration, as a side effect of
the therapeutic relationship. The therapist is often the
recipient of his patients' expectations of finding some-

one who will fill all of their unmet needs—sexual, nurturing, understanding, etc. Obviously, the therapist can not meet these expectations. Disappointment frequently leads the patient to feel and then express toward the therapist all of the pent-up rage from similar disappointments at the hands of parents in childhood.

And, of course, the therapist cannot gratify his own needs, sexual or otherwise, with his patients. He is free to do so in marriage. He enjoys complete control. He has a willing subject who flatters him, feeds his need to be admired, is dependent on him in such a special way that no rival, no matter how attractive, could possibly compete. He does not have to worry any more about being opposed, being overruled (as by his patients, his own analyst, and his supervisors). He cannot be abandoned, any more than he could if he were the only supplier of heroin to an addict. For the first time in his life, the therapist can feel secure. He will always have a loving, adoring person near him who will see things his way and never criticize him. With this kind of relationship, sex is usually fantastic; any anxieties or insecurities in this area are covered over by the glow of perfect union.

In fact, the bliss often lasts for quite a while. Sometimes it begins to erode after a few months, but sometimes it lasts for several years. Yet it is obvious that this arrangement contains within it the seeds of its own destruction—a truly built-in obsolescence. Let me mention a few examples that I have encountered in my practice, disguised to avoid identification.

1. Alma is a very bright, dynamic, creative woman in her late thirties. She was a success as a film editor, before shifting to training as a psychotherapist. As talented in therapy as she had been as a film editor, she was extraordinarily successful within a short time. Harold, her husband of several years, is an intelligent, attractive and pleasant man, but he has a poor self-image and obviously picked Alma—with her talent, fine mind, and charisma—in part as a narcissistic

extension for him. Though he started with a successful business, he was unable to sustain this success in the course of their marriage. Alma always supplied most of the money, ideas and direction in the marriage. After his business lagged, Alma induced him to follow her into the field of therapy. Always a couple of years behind her in training, he fell even farther behind in achievement. Alma had completely outclassed and outstripped him again. Her practice was flourishing while his did not. When I first saw Alma, she was complaining that she was depressed about being constantly deprived. She always had to shoulder all the burdens—her mother (whom she still supported) and her husband and her children. Why did she always end up being the responsible one? Why did she always have to make all the decisions? Why didn't anyone ever take care of her? At first it sounded as if Alma just had the misfortune to marry a "loser." But then she joined a therapy group. Within a short time, she became the "den mother"—actually, the group goddess—and was taking care of everyone. She was bossy, but usually kindly. Then she began to complain that no one in the group ever gave her any attention, that she was always responsive to others but no one cared about her. The group was quick to point out that she had positioned herself as the mother and had never asked for anything. Gradually, but with great difficulty, she began to communicate her needs. When she did, she invariably got response, but it was difficult for her not to slide back into her mothering role. Gradually, she is beginning to understand that her problem is *not* that she just happened to marry a "loser"; she set herself up to be a narcissistic extension for her husband. She is beginning to ask for more from her husband and, after an initial revolt, he is beginning to respond. It is a long, difficult struggle to undo a pattern of several years' duration, but their relationship has improved considerably.

2. Dave is a respected psychotherapist. When he met Ellen, he had been divorced for five years. Ellen

had carved out a fairly successful career as a social worker. She, too, had been divorced for a few years. She had her own apartment, her own circle of friends, and was leading a life that was satisfying, if somewhat lacking in a consistent intimate relationship. When Dave came along, he fell madly in love with her and she with him. They found in each other the closeness and warmth that had been missing in their lives. At first, their marriage was ideal. Then, gradually, Dave began to assert his strength, to try to be the omnipotent, admired one in the relationship, a narcissistic extension for Ellen. Subtly, and then not so subtly, he put Ellen down for not being as free and creative and involved as he was. He belittled her job as a social worker and said she should get analytic training; he teased her for not being as outgoing as he was. Dave began to play God in the relationship. Ellen's agency closed down and she was out of a job. Though she intended to find another one immediately, somehow she never got around to it. She had made Dave into a narcissistic extension, as unconsciously he had planned for her to do. She spent the next two years essentially vegetating at home. She hated cooking and housework, so she did little of either; she rarely saw her friends and she drifted into a state of mere existence. Her husband and her friends became concerned over her lack of drive, but Ellen claimed that was the way she wanted it. Finally Dave stopped being sympathetic. He became outright angry at having to support Ellen and getting nothing in return from her. At his insistence and that of her friends, she went into therapy, but the inequality in the relationship persisted. Dave felt more and more cheated, and finally he left Ellen. Almost immediately afterwards, Ellen got another good job, received promotions, and went back to being the autonomous, self-supporting, reasonably involved person she had been before meeting Dave. As for Dave, he got himself another girl and then another wife, and repeated with her the pattern of God-like domination. Now he is beginning to see how he engineers the very situation that so distresses him. He is trying very hard not to do it again; his current marriage appears to have a better prognosis.

3. When Jim first met Al, Jim was going to school and Al was a very successful businessman. They had a close, consistent homosexual relationship, spending a great deal of time with one another. When Jim was in financial trouble, he would often get help from Al who was quite affluent and very loving. Jim was attending school with the goal of becoming a psychotherapist. He was enormously bright and talented in this field and wanted to move to a larger city where he could get further training and establish a good practice. He induced Al to sell his business and move with him. Once on Jim's home territory, Al spent the next three years without earning a cent. He was completely dominated by Jim's charismatic, God-like personality; he had no friends who were not in Jim's circle and he ceased to work at any job that employed him gainfully. His personality became more and more submerged. He had little to say to Jim, merely making a narcissistic extension of him and living through him. Finally Jim began complaining about the dullness and one-sidedness of their relationship. Very gradually Al began, through therapy, to see how he had practically ceased to exist as a person in his own right. They are both in therapy now—both seeing their mutual role in the disastrous erosion of their relationship, both trying to make changes so that it can continue and become more satisfying. Jim is growing aware of how he invariably takes over anyone—including his therapist—with his wit, charm, and brilliance, and how difficult it is for him to allow anyone to give him anything. Al is understanding more and more clearly how drastically he let go of his autonomy and lived through Jim as an extension; he is attempting to reinforce himself as a separate person. Both of them are committed to their relationship with each other because of basic feelings of love, trust, and

respect. It will be a difficult task, but the outlook for their relationship seems quite good.

I have spent many hours for many years listening to the therapist's side of the story (and, parenthetically, to my own, for I am a therapist with the same occupational disease). What happens to us therapists? After a while, we begin to feel drained and cheated. I used to complain that I saw out-patients all week long, and then had an in-patient on my hands every weekend. After a whole day of listening to other people and denying myself, who wanted to come home to more of that? It was my occupational choice to be everybody's parent, but what about *my* needs? Wasn't I ever going to be taken care of, listened to, allowed to be dependent? When I tried that, my wife yelled—that wasn't part of the contract. In truth, it wasn't. I had really promised to be the perennial parent and narcissistic extension for her. She wasn't wrong in reminding me of that. But, I protested, it was an unfair contract. I didn't realize what I was doing. I was carried away by my own grandiosity. Now what? I really *was* being deprived. If my feelings didn't tell me, my ulcer did.

I began to feel angry and depressed. I began to push her to be more autonomous and independent. Of course, I was *commanding* her to become more autonomous. The slight contradiction in this eluded me. But what could I do now? What I usually did was tell her to get a therapist of her own. I no longer wanted to be her therapist. Being knowledgeable about the field, I helped her make the choice. When she came back and inevitably reported what went on in the sessions, I conveyed, subtly or not so subtly, that her therapist was not really dealing with her problem correctly—as, of course, I could do. So I kept my grandiose role and my control over the measure that I hoped was going to get me off the hook of constantly having to be in control. Now what? After a while, we both decided it would be better if she didn't discuss with me what went on in her therapy. At least my roster of patients was reduced by one.

Over the years, my case load, when it did not consist mostly of therapists, consisted of many of their mates. I began to wonder, at one point, if we therapists might not have a totally closed system, consisting of treating only one another and our mates. We wouldn't have to admit any strangers at all and we could all flourish. It would be like a chain-letter, everyone gets rich and nobody loses. Sending my wife—and often myself—to a therapist worked up to a point, if, unconsciously, I hadn't made sure that I wouldn't be referring her to a therapist who couldn't really threaten my exalted position in her eyes.

So the bliss ends, and it ends in a sea of unfulfilled promises, deprivation, anger, and self-pity for the therapist. Building something substantial out of the rubble of this unfortunate system is no mean task.

But how about the mates? In some ways, their plight is more devastating than the therapist's. Let me give two examples:

1. Esther was the wife of a well-known therapist. When he married her, she had a rather menial position and was surprised at his interest in her. She was quite attractive and relatively bright, but she only had a high-school education and no special sophistication. Undoubtedly he married her because he did not see himself as particularly attractive, so she, being very beautiful, was a narcissistic extension for him. And she married him because he was a narcissistic extension for her. Their marriage was happy at first and they had three children. He was always the complete lord and master in the home, and this seemed perfectly appropriate to her. Her parents were first-generation immigrants and she had been brought up to take a subordinate position in relation to her husband. But as he began to be successful and even somewhat famous, and to travel in sophisticated circles, he became increasingly critical of her and excluded her from his life.

Ultimately, this led to bitter arguments and violent scenes between them; finally her husband asked for a divorce. Esther felt crushed: after fifteen years of marriage, during which she was devoted to her husband, doing her utmost to comply with all his requests and trying to become the kind of person he wanted, she was now being discarded like an old shoe. This led to a depression that brought her to seek psychiatric help.

2. Joan had been a patient of Dan's for a year when he told her that he was very much interested in her as a woman, that he had serious intentions toward her, and that he wanted to terminate their patient-therapist relationship and change it into a social one. He volunteered to recommend another therapist, in case she decided to continue treatment, but she refused this. Joan had always been very fond of Dan and she was delighted to change the nature of their relationship. She had idealized him when he was the therapist. Within a very short time, they were very much in love with one another and after another brief interval they decided to marry. Their marriage was an extraordinarily close and happy one for the first two years. However, in many ways Dan continued to act as Joan's therapist and as a narcissistic extension for her. She became increasingly unsure of herself, frequently anxious and depressed, and Dan became increasingly intolerant of having to bail her out. Finally they decided she should go back into therapy. This helped to some degree, and presently they are trying to establish a working relationship, but Joan is hardly as happy or secure as she had been at the beginning of the marriage.

Very frequently, under the illusion of perpetual, unfailing care, the mates give up their autonomy and sink into positions of helplessness and inability to cope with their inner problems or with reality. They try to set up their mates as narcissistic extensions to fill voids they feel in themselves. Then, when their therapist-mates begin to want some strength and support from them, they find that they are truly unable to give it. They are also outraged by this demand, feeling suddenly attacked for a position that was not only offered freely to them but practically forced upon them, and constantly reinforced by their therapist-mates. After months or years of being rewarded for dependency, loss of autonomy, and regression, they are now accused of having become "vegetables," and not very nourishing vegetables at that. Their mates no longer want to hear their complaints, no longer want to "cure" them. Where can they go? Only to another therapist. And so the game continues, except that it is musical couches, instead of musical chairs.

I have tried to illustrate what I have found to be a common occupational disease of therapists. It seems to matter not whether the therapist is male or female, heterosexual or homosexual, Jewish or Italian (is there anything else?). I wish I had a cure for the disease, but I believe I have exhausted all of my own omnipotence on my mates! One attempt at a solution, frequently made, is that the therapist's mate, in self-defense, and also at the instigation of the therapist, seeks a career in the field of therapy in his or her own right. Another solution might be to pass a law that therapists can live only with other therapists! But does this merely substitute new problems for the old ones? Do we now have a battle of two grandiose people? It would be interesting to see how unions between therapists of essentially equal stature work out. There *I* go, still trying to be omniscient. I thought I had just decided to leave the solution to someone else. Perhaps my wife?

Anyway, we can see that relationships between mates, one or both of whom are chosen mainly as narcissistic extensions, do not turn out very well. If you are still free to choose a mate, you might do well to examine whether you are choosing yours because he or she seems to fill some void in your own self-esteem, rather than because they are kind, reliable, interesting, emotionally responsive people. If you have made a succession of poor choices of mate, it may be especially important for you to be aware of this pitfall. And don't forget that this rule—not relating to people, and not letting them relate to you, on the basis of narcissistic extension—applies as well to friends, children, and parents.

CHAPTER 12

A Chronological Examination of Issues of Self-esteem

One way to approach an understanding of the problems we may have in our ability to feel good about ourselves is to examine the various issues in our self-esteem system at the different stages of our lives, starting from the time we are born.

1. *Babyhood*

Let us begin from scratch—from birth. Most mothers will feel that their babies are absolutely adorable. The special gleam in their eyes when responding to them will give the baby a feeling of being special, which he will carry with him throughout his life. This positive reflection in his mother's eyes will give the baby a fine start in his ability to feel good about himself.

Some mothers, for a variety of reasons, may not see their babies as beautiful and adorable. They may project negative images they have of themselves onto the baby. Unconsciously they may see the baby as resembling someone in their own or their husband's family whom they dislike. In this case, they may not only fail to mirror admiration and adoration, but may actually reflect disappointment and disparagement, and even hostility and rejection. Perhaps they will not acknowledge their feelings, but they may at least have a dim awareness of them. They may convey their disapproval to the baby even if they are not conscious of it, and even if they employ a defense. They may even say their baby is beautiful, though they do not really believe it. Of course, most mothers believe their baby is the most beautiful in the world. Their adoration is not based on physical beauty alone, but on the total person of the baby. The infant may be utterly delightful, sweet, and lovable, despite a lack of outstanding physical beauty. If you look at your baby and from the beginning feel a sense of disappointment in his physical appearance or his total self, then perhaps you *are* one of those mothers who is unable to give what is required. You cannot really change how you feel, but you can try to modify it and try to behave accordingly. You know that how the baby is reflected in your eyes is crucial to the development of his self-esteem, so crucial itself to a great many other issues in his future.

One of my relatives tells how her mother always made fun of what an ugly baby she was. She used to remark, "The only good thing I could say was, 'Well, at least you're healthy.' " My relative, who grew up to be very attractive, maintained a negative view of her physical self until she went into therapy and married a man who reinforced a positive self-image. Another lesson to be learned from this anecdote is that if you do have a negative response to the physical aspect of your baby, you may not be totally able to control your non-verbal responses, but at least you can certainly avoid verbalizing and especially repeating negative responses. You cannot be responsible for what you *feel*, but you certainly can be responsible for what you say and do. Negative verbal responses—or even exaggerated and conscious non-verbal negative responses—to your baby and later to your child are destructive and should be avoided as much as possible. These negative responses can also damage the child's intellectual ability, emotions, manual dexterity, and ability to cope with other problems.

Some mothers and fathers develop immediate responses to the way their baby looks—not so much in terms of their beauty or lack of it, but in terms of whom they resemble. If you think you're wonderful and beautiful and the baby "looks just like me," either in objective reality or in your subjective reality, then the baby is a "chip off the old block" and in luck. But suppose your baby has the misfortune to look exactly like your mother-in-law, and you happen to hate your mother-in-law. (Remember the old joke about the definition of mixed emotions—watching your mother-in-law drive off a cliff in your brand-new Cadillac?) Well, if you think your baby looks like your mother-in-law, or your sister or brother or mother or father, whom you consciously or unconsciously detest, then that poor baby may become the instant repository for all the negative feelings you have had or may now have toward the original figure. I have treated many patients whose mothers responded exactly like that. They would even call the child, throughout his life, by the name of the hated sister or brother. This makes it almost impossible to love the baby without some deep self-scrutiny or perhaps outside professional help.

One patient I had said her mother continually slipped and called her by the name of a hated younger sister of whom the mother was enormously jealous. This patient felt that her mother had never loved her and, in fact, had always been destructive to her. I interviewed the mother of the patient who confirmed the truth of this. Because of the resemblance to the younger sister, she had never been able to feel the same sort of love toward this daughter that she felt toward her other children. Feeling enormously guilty about it, she had tried to compensate by favoring the daughter in certain ways, but this had only resulted in an even more confusing situation for the daughter, and between the daughter and her siblings. The siblings were always angry because she was favored, so she ended up losing their love and support, as well as her mother's. If you, as a parent, are aware of this kind of immediate negative reaction to your baby, try to do some soul-searching to help erase it.

This soul-searching may help you become more conscious of your projecting another person's identity onto your child. This, in turn, may help you disentangle the child from the person you are projecting, so that you can respond to him as the person he actually is. If this doesn't work, you should seek professional help as soon as possible, before too much damage is done.

Special problems in relating to a baby can occur if you are unfortunate enough to have a handicapped child. Among the more common handicaps are mental retardation, childhood schizophrenia, infantile autism, crossed eyes, blindness, deafness, cerebral palsy, anatomical defects from hereditary causes, or birth defects. Parents—especially mothers—of these children often have major difficulties in relating to them. They will perceive the bearing of such a child as a severe narcissistic wound. Of course, the higher the mother's level of self-esteem the better she will be able to cope with this wound. Any mother, to some degree, experiences a child as a narcissistic extension of her own body. If the mother has problems about her own body image (as so many of us do), then the handicapped child represents a destruction of part of this image. The unconscious result of this is a feeling of rage, both against fate and against the child. Since this feeling of rage against the child is totally unacceptable to the conscious part of the mind, it invariably produces guilt. In many cases, the rage is repressed through the overt expression of overconcern and overprotectiveness. What often happens—and is really injurious to the handicapped child—is that the mother will go out of her way to favor him. In overprotecting him, she may make him into a psychological invalid, in addition to his having a physical or mental handicap. The healthiest attitude is one of honest acceptance of the handicap—giving any real help the handicap requires but, beyond this, treating the child normally. Often, the parent's self-image, wounded by extension, so regularly interferes with this process that it is worthwhile to get counseling help from one of the organizations that deal with handicapped children, such as United Cerebral Palsy, the Muscular Dystrophy Association, and others. The problems can extend beyond the mother and child, often having a major effect on the siblings in the family. These siblings are caught among conflicting emotions. There is anger at the unequal attention the handicapped child receives, and awareness of the mother's unconscious hostility toward the handicapped child. There is their own guilt for anger at getting less than their share of attention, and their genuine love and concern for their handicapped sibling. This is quite a load for children to bear and can often result in serious emotional problems—and all the more reason for the parents regularly to seek some kind of counseling.

To return to the more general issue of reactions to babies, there must be a very strong tendency in all of us to project our grandiosity on the newborn or the baby. Why else all the paintings of the Madonna and Child or of the baby Buddha? Why the Adoration of the Magi? A child must represent for us the repository of our unfulfilled potential, the perfect subject for our projections of our grandiose selves. We adore a child for what it is and what it will become. It has to do nothing, prove nothing, perform not at all in order to be the recipient of our adoration. This is what we would have wanted as babies—to get total, unconditional adoration. The baby needs this, and very many of us did not get it when *we* were babies. So we project our own unfulfilled baby selves on The Baby and get vicariously what we missed out on at that specific phase of our development. Our reactions of love and adoration of babies represent an opportunity for us to experience vicariously what we needed when *we* were babies. It also hints broadly that almost all of us still need that same kind of reaction as adults from the people around us. We must remember that we *can* still get it; it is not too late. If we ask for what we need in terms of enhancement of our self-esteem, and sensibly seek out the people around us who are ready, willing, and able to give it to us, we can do a great deal more to make up for whatever deficits we experienced when we were babies.

2. *Childhood*

There are two different kinds of self-esteem problems that we can experience in childhood—one involves not getting enough reflection of admiration and love, and another results from getting too much admiration. Though there may be no such thing as too much during the first year or two, there are certainly problems from the third year on that arise from getting too much admiration.

Not much needs to be said any longer about a child's need for sufficient admiration. We all understand that if he is never praised for his talents, physical and emotional qualities, and real accomplishments, he will grow up *feeling* he is a nothing, that he just does not count. No matter how good he looks, how well he performs as an adult, he will not recognize that as part of himself.

I have a patient who said, "When I was in my early twenties, there was some guy who was first in his class at college, the quarterback on the football team, did very well with women, and was the leading vocalist in the glee club. But it wasn't me. I was completely cut off from him. I still felt that the basic me was an absolute zero." This particular patient had been totally wiped out by two very self-centered parents and three very jealous siblings. The family treated him like the class dunce and the village idiot. He was told he should be seen and not heard, and not seen too often at that. What formed his self-image was what was reflected from his nuclear family. During his childhood, his accomplishments were recognized at school but never at home. Grown, he was never able to internalize praise and admiration. The lesson we must all learn from this is to try to *say* anything good you really feel about a child. Being proud of him, or boasting to the neighbors about him, does not do *him* any good. He has to hear it from you. You will do him a lot more good by contributing to his bank account of self-esteem than you will by taking out a trust fund for him. The dividends and interest on the former are infinitely higher.

Problems that result from lack of enhancement of self-love in childhood are almost truisms and cliches in today's world. The problems *I* find more challenging—because they have only recently become the subject of psychoanalytic attention—are those that derive from children getting *too* much attention. Why is it that a child star like Judy Garland, who got so much admiration and attention during her childhood, had such serious emotional problems? Musical child prodigy Oscar Levant was another example of a man with many psychological problems. Child chess genius, Bobby Fischer, is known to be extremely difficult and troubled. Many of my patients who have severe problems with their self-image were particularly beautiful, rich, talented, or bright as children. They developed a picture of themselves as privileged, extraordinary, superhuman people. I have presented some examples of people like this (Peggy and Len in Ch. VI), for whom it was difficult to tolerate the ordinary vicissitudes and disappointments of life.

One of my patients wrote about his childhood, and that of some of his friends. "Our parents built their lives around us. They set themselves up to serve our needs completely. We were tiny giants, swathed in a dream of lifelong Eden. The world was soft and nourishing, with us at the center. We barely began to cry or complain, and food was on the way. We were carefully protected from the consequences of our own actions. For example, I knew that if I lost any money, my father would give it right back to me. It was only fair. At eight or nine, I realized my mother just couldn't make me cry; her anger was unconvincing. I knew she would back down in any fight because at heart she wanted me to win. Then she could praise me for being so forceful and determined. When I really needed determination, say, in building a tricky model airplane, I got the message that only a fool (later on—a masochist) would put up with so much frustration. Thank God that college takes many of us away from home. Maybe by the time we're twenty, reality has intruded enough to shake our faith that the whole world loves us as our parents did. Where's our attentive audience? Why can't they see how important we are? There must be a trick. We imagine ourselves as magical Peter Pan angel artists. Or better yet, world saviors—rock musicians remaking the universe with a million-amp twitch, Tim Leary tweaking everyone's DNA, or my friend, David, who will be Omnipotent Pope Emperor Che Mao Lord Christ Gautama of the Universe or nothing, zero, nil. So he can't get it together to carve out a career as world savior. He just can't get those graduate school applications in the mail."

What my patient is talking about is the absence of realistic curbs put upon his grandiosity. He was brought up to think he could get everything he wanted, just by willing it. When he had to struggle to achieve a goal, as most of us in fact do, he had not learned how. He had the fantasy, and the conditioning, that led him to believe in his own omnipotence, and this made him unable to hustle to get what he wanted. Getting too much adoration and indulgence, having no realistic limits, and being treated too much as a very special person, can be as destructive in many ways during childhood as getting too little during our first two years. As we have seen from the examples of uncurbed power leading to destructive grandiosity (Hitler, Mussolini, and Amin), giving a child too much license without enough limits can cause major, even tragic problems for them.

Sometimes I have serious reservations even about children attending private schools. The private-school child may grow up feeling that he is a member of an elite and may have difficulty meeting challenges or enduring frustrations and disappointments. Did Judy Gar-

land and Oscar Levant make repeated suicide attempts
because they felt so special that they were enraged
when the ordinary circumstances of life frustrated them
and punctured the balloon of their grandiosity? Is this
what happened to Freddie Prinze? In my experience, I
have seen many patients whose suicide attempts were
based precisely on this dynamic.

Dan was brought up as a child genius. This was conveyed to him literally. The school psychologist, who
was a friend of his father, gave him an I.Q. test when
he was five years old. He achieved the highest score of
any client she had ever had. This news was transmitted
to Dan's father, and subsequently to little Dan. Even
before then, he had received accolades for telling time
at age two, reading at age three, reciting poetry and
then even writing it at ages five and six. He was sent to
a very fine, elite private school and quickly became the
school's resident child genius. In his junior-high-school,
high-school, college, and graduate-school years, he
went to special schools for geniuses. He was always
first in his class . . . until college. There, with the nar-
rowing by selection, he was competing with other similarly endowed students. He found the competition too
challenging and withdrew from it, just managing to get
by with fair, but not outstanding, grades.

His academic success was paralleled by his prowess
with women. He was extraordinarily successful sexually, and whatever peer admiration he lost by his failure to continue his outstanding academic achievement,
he gained from his sexual proficiency. He received the
nickname of "Superstud" from his admiring fellows.
Among his female conquests was one young woman
who was not particularly beautiful or intelligent or sophisticated. Dan went out with her a few times with
some success. Then she began to appear to reject him.
Reject *him*? How could that happen? All his friends
were in on the details of his affair with her. His reputation as "Superstud" could certainly not be injured by
failing with her. Yet she stood him up on a date—she
just never appeared. Dan was furious, but he was also

destroyed. He had gone from grandiosity to humiliation and mortification in one fell swoop. How could that inconsequential little nothing shoot *him* down? Perhaps he wasn't as great as he thought. The next morning Dan made a serious suicide attempt. He was saved from dying only by the most fortuitous and unexpected circumstances. Neither he nor his analyst could really understand the reason for the attempt. It was only years later, with our expanded knowledge about narcissism, grandiosity, and humiliation, that the reason for the attempt became clear. He had gone from hero to zero, and he could not bear the sudden drop in his self-esteem, or the humiliation of others knowing about his failure.

So in contrast to infancy, when you can err only through not giving a baby enough adoration, in childhood there has to be a balance between a great deal of praise for real accomplishments and limits on a child's grandiosity. This may be a special problem for extraordinarily rich, beautiful, or talented children; ordinary children may not have the worry. Yet, if you treat your ordinary child as if he is the world's greatest genius or a highly privileged character, you *can* create the same problem in him. The responses he gets later on from the world will not parallel your response to him. The change will be jarring. Children need a great deal of praise, but certain limits on their grandiosity.

3. *Adolescence*

Adolescence is a time when young men and women are especially focused on their physical appearance. Their self-image, as with almost everything else in their lives, is subject to all kinds of wild fluctuations, from very high to very low. Adolescence is a period of tremendous flux and instability. One of the most sensitive issues around self-esteem has to do with whether the adolescent is an early bloomer or a late bloomer. Either extreme seems to be fraught with wounds to the young person's self-image. If a girl begins to develop breasts and pubic hair before her peers, she feels very self-conscious, as if she is a freak. If, on the other hand, she doesn't develop at a time when most of her friends do, she fears that there is something seriously wrong with her femininity and wonders whether she will ever be "normal." The same applies to boys and the development of facial and body hair.

Fourteen seems to be an age at which girls—boys, also, but to a lesser degree—are extremely absorbed by their physical appearance. I remember that one of my daughters seemed constantly to be in the bathroom between the ages of fourteen and fifteen. She took endless showers, and the sound of the hair dryer was always assaulting my ears. Her face was always covered with zinc oxide to prevent or cure an acne condition that was invisible to me, and that I still think was more imagined than real. Acne, of course, *can* be the scourge of adolescence. Many adolescents develop it at a time when they are paying enormous attention to their body image. Every pimple takes on the proportions of a huge mountain, and they experience themselves as one giant pimple. They feel ugly and disgusting even if they have the mildest condition. On the other hand, they can have periods of grandiosity about their irresistibility and attractiveness. They may flaunt their budding sexuality in the most outrageous ways, yet inwardly feeling frightened and insecure about their appearance and their gender identity. Identity itself is certainly an important word that comes to mind concerning adolescence, and one of the crucial issues of identity is gender identity. "Am I a real man or a real woman?" "How come my breasts are so small when Sally's are so well-developed?" "Johnny has been shaving for a year and I don't even have any fuzz. I wonder if there's something wrong with me. Maybe I'm a homosexual. My penis doesn't seem to be as big as the other fellows'. I wonder if girls will ever like me?"

Adolescence is a period when it is extremely important to receive reinforcement about one's attractiveness. A most important aid is when the parent of the opposite sex can get past incest fears in order to openly acknowledge admiration for the budding young adolescent. Being attracted to one's adolescent child of the opposite sex is, as we've seen, a perfectly normal phenomenon. Sharing this reaction with the adolescent can go a long way to help develop a positive feeling about gender identity and general attractiveness. Many parents, especially fathers, are made anxious by their feelings of sexual interest in and attraction for their daughters. Instead of accepting these feelings and sharing them, the fathers' anxiety over them can lead to a total rejection and avoidance of their teen-age daughters. This distancing is interpreted by daughters as a rejection of their sexual selves because of imagined unattractiveness, and can do a great deal of damage to their self-image at a time in life when they most need their attractiveness affirmed. The same situation occurs between mothers and sons, but is somewhat less striking. Between fathers and adolescent daughters, there are sometimes periods that may extend for years during which their communication is minimal.

Another special feature of adolescence is blushing. Blushing is really a symptom characteristic of an inner conflict between exhibitionism and feelings of embarrassment. The blush which makes the face go red is clearly an unconscious way of calling attention to oneself. It often accompanies a feeling connected either with sex or with wanting attention and admiration. While the face is turning red as if to say, "Hey, look at me," this phenomenon is accompanied by an excruciatingly painful feeling of mortification. It incorporates the "crime" of vanity with the most dreaded punishment for it—public humiliation. Of course, blushing can and does occasionally occur before and frequently after adolescence, but it is especially prevalent at this time, when there are such pronounced swings in self-esteem and conflicts about wanting to be admired.

Adolescence is, of course, also the period during which sex "rears its ugly head" and dating begins. Adolescents put special emphasis on their own and their partners' physical beauty. They are merciless in ridiculing themselves, their friends, and their partners over physical defects, real or imagined. Prone to choose partners who enhance them as narcissistic extensions, the girls will pursue the most handsome boy or the football hero, and the boys will eye the beauty queen. Other qualities—character, intelligence, integrity—run a very poor second to external appearance. Forgetting this, parents are often shocked at the choices their adolescents make. Since self-image and narcissistic extension are so important to adolescents, parents should try to remember that the choices their children make during those years are not necessarily the ones they will make when their feelings of their own attractiveness as people and their security about their gender identity are more certain and fixed. Adolescent crushes are vivid examples of projections of grandiosity onto some unattainable figure—the high-school football hero, a teacher, a rock star, a movie idol. This figure is then worshiped as if he were a god. In successive generations, girls have fainted during performances by Frank Sinatra, Elvis Presley, the Beatles, and Elton John. Adolescent boys often project their grandiosity onto some sports hero like Babe Ruth, Henry Aaron, or Muhammad Ali.

I don't see how I ever got through my adolescence, and I would certainly never want to go through it again! I had no sense of my intelligence, attractiveness, or competence. My self-esteem would fluctuate from way up to way down. I was constantly concerned about acne and about whether I would ever get a date. I had no idea of my sexual adequacy or total lack of it. Perhaps, in dealing with adolescents, we can try to recall our own adolescence and remember the experiences we had that reinforced our self-esteem and were so welcome and so necessary at that time of our lives.

And aside from all of the problems that come from low self-esteem, we have to remember that adolescent athletic heroes or beauty queens or movie stars like Elizabeth Taylor and Mickey Rooney can face all kinds of problems dealing with their grandiosity, problems that, as we have seen, can lead to instability and unhappiness in adult life. So realistic limits must be set during this age period, too.

4. *Marriage*

Many of the important issues in the choice of marriage partners have been dealt with in the section on narcissistic extensions. Do you choose someone to marry because he or she looks good on your arm and therefore your stature is enhanced? Or do you choose someone toward whom you feel a kinship, a warmth, a closeness? A good friend of mine went out with a woman and said to her on their first date, "You are exactly the right woman for me to marry. You are beautiful, intelligent, well-educated, cultured, and would make an excellent wife, hostess, and mother." Despite his intellectual knowledge that she would enhance his image tremendously, he did not feel a real closeness or emotional connection to her. Subsequently, he did marry her. And, despite all of her assets, which he truly appreciated, he could never really feel intense love for her. Eventually the marriage ended in divorce. He had made a choice on the basis of her value as a narcissistic extension for him, but he did not really love her.

During a marriage, it is important to remember that *your mate is a separate person from you*. What he or she does, or fails to do, is not really a reflection on you. Many people feel either too much pride or too much shame about some quality that their mate may possess. They may try to live through their mate—in reflected glory—and will almost surely be disappointed, even if that mate is an outstanding success. Or they will be constantly ashamed and embarrassed by real or fancied deficiencies in a mate. Living through one's mate does very little for one's self-esteem for any real length of time. There may be an immediate, short-term gain through narcissistic extension, for instance, in

marrying a wealthy or prominent or beautiful partner.
But living in his or her shadow eventually diminishes
one's self-esteem, rather than enhancing it. And this
process often produces envy and anger, not continual,
ungrudging admiration for a more prominent, attractive, or charismatic mate. The other problem—being
ashamed of one's mate—is a very sad one, especially if
that mate is privately pleasing. How the one you
choose looks on your arm or to the outside world is
relatively unimportant, compared to whether he or she
makes *you* happy. Sometimes this overconcern about a
mate's lack of beauty or financial success, or some
physical or emotional defect, can erode a good relationship. This may be based, at least in part, on a grandiose image of one's self and a need for the same
perfection in a mate. Putting down one's mate may
stem from a need to feel secure from abandonment. By
feeling superior to a mate, a person may reassure himself that he is so much more valuable than his partner
that there is no way for him or her to consider a
replacement.

The problems parents can face in the relationship
with their babies and children, when they turn them
into negative narcissistic extensions of themselves, has
been dealt with in some detail in the part of this chapter dealing with babies. However, there is another
problem concerning narcissistic extension that can be
equally destructive: when we assign to our children the
task of fulfilling our own thwarted ambitions, putting a
burden on them to carry out this assignment. Be sure
your son really wants to be a star athlete for himself,
not because you are pushing him to do something you
always fantasized for yourself but never succeeded in
accomplishing. The typical stage mother is an example
of this. And it is best to be wary about pushing your
child into playing an instrument, or singing or painting
or becoming a doctor. It may be something you want
him to do, either because you cannot do it yourself or
you think it will add to your own image and glory.

I have a patient who pushed her son into becoming a doctor. He managed to get through college, medical school, internship, and residency, but finally realized his mistake, quit, and went into business. I have another patient whose father decided he should be an engineer. The boy got his degree, hating every minute of it, but later became an actor's agent.

To sum up, you must try to enhance your self-esteem by your own accomplishments, getting praise for these, *not* through the accomplishments of your mate or children. The latter approach invariably backfires. Even if your mate or children achieve exactly as you want them to—which you can't and shouldn't count on—you cannot get much ongoing mileage for yourself out of what *they do*. They aren't *you*. You need to get your own credit for your own accomplishments.

5. *Middle Age*

There is an old joke about middle age being five years older than you are. Actually, the feeling of being middle-aged does not arrive at the same chronological time for everyone. Many people resist, even deny the reality that they are losing some of their attractiveness, physical strength, athletic ability, sexual power, sense of adventure and, perhaps, even creativity. Many women become very upset at the appearance of wrinkles on their faces and a flabbiness in their figures. Men also worry about wrinkles, baldness, and the appearance of a potbelly. Beyond these relatively minor blows to self-esteem and the difficulty of adjusting to them, major depressions may occur in women around the age of the menopause (in the early fifties) and, less frequently, in men in the early sixties. These are called menopausal or involutional depressions; they have an obvious relationship to a lowering of narcissistic reflections. A person who has rested a great deal of his self-esteem on those aspects of personality—on appearance or strength—that, in fact, do begin to fade with age may have a difficult time adjusting.

In his play, *The Master Builder*, Ibsen describes a man going through such an adjustment. Philippe Halsman, in an interview that appears later in this book, talks of the "Phenomenon of the Lost Image"—that people continue to see themselves physically as they were in their forties or fifties, but never older than that. Perhaps one way of handling the loss of some power, strength, sexuality, and attractiveness is to feel that one has gained in wisdom about the world more than he has lost in other areas.

This might lead us to the conclusion that those who have placed value all through their lives on such attributes as wisdom, character, personality, ability to communicate, and even money, which may increase rather than diminish with age, are fortunate. Able to experience the aging process without so much loss of self-esteem, they may even experience an increase in certain instances—an idea that might have some ramifications of the kinds of things we teach ourselves and our children to value. Here we may have to try to counter the effects of important forces in our culture—television, advertising, movies, theater—which tend to place emphasis on physical appearance and physical strength, the very things that tend to diminish with age. Being able to face middle age gracefully, without too great a loss in self-esteem or too great an envy of youth, is a difficult adjustment, but one that can be managed with awareness of the issues involved.

6. *Old Age*

Old age is, of course, even more difficult to handle than middle age in terms of self-esteem. Sophie Tucker, the comedienne, once said, "Up until eighteen, you need good parents. From eighteen to thirty-five, you need good looks. From thirty-five to fifty you need a good personality. And after fifty you need money." There is probably more truth in her statement than most of us would like to believe. In fact, old people have a tremendous preoccupation with money. When our looks, often our health, our strength, our sexual power, our earning power, and our ability to interest other people are failing rapidly, it is extremely difficult for us to maintain a strong, positive image of ourselves. Some of it remains through reminiscences of earlier triumphs and days of glory. (Older people have a tendency to repeat stories of their youth over and over again.) In some societies, older people are revered, but unfortunately rarely in our own.

I think it is very wise—seriously—to follow Sophie Tucker's advice and to be sure that you are as well provided for financially as possible. Money is power and does add to our self-esteem. The more we have of it in our old age, the better off we are. Also, hopefully, if we have established good relationships with mates, friends, and children, they will support us when we really need them. To be old, poor, and friendless is a sad position. The scenes that have emerged from recent investigations of nursing homes should serve as adequate warning and prompt us to think ahead, providing as many support systems as we can against this most difficult period, in which the raids on our self-esteem are many.

Our success in dealing with old age, however, will depend even more upon how strongly we have built up a solid core of self-esteem. True, money will help, but the greatest old-age insurance policy in the world will be a healthy feeling of self-love that can resist all of the stings, crises, failures in health, loss of loved ones and power and attractiveness. If we have been fortified with the necessary amount of positive reflection in our childhood and have been able to take in deserved praise for our successes, we will indeed be fortunate. However, if we have had interferences in our self-esteem system, the sooner we try to repair them—such as by reading this book and trying to heed its advice—the better off we are. Now is the time to undo your horizontal and vertical splits, so you will be able to take in praise for accomplishments and add to your level of self-esteem. Now is the time to admit your grandiose fantasies, so you will be less afraid to have a healthy appreciation of yourself. And now is the time to learn to do what will get you rewards of admiration from people who can appreciate you, and how to be able to take in this admiration. All of this will gradually build up your self-esteem. While not neglecting your real bank account, your bank account of self-esteem will turn out to be an even more important insurance policy in helping you to weather the depletions and losses that accompany old age.

CHAPTER 13

An Interview with Philippe Halsman, the Portrait Photographer, About Self-image

In writing a book about our self-esteem and our image of ourselves, I thought it would be appropriate to interview Philippe Halsman, probably the world's most illustrious portrait photographer. Mr. Halsman has taken photographs of many of the world's leading figures and he has written two books, *Sight and Insight* and *The Jump Book—Interpreting the Jumps of People*. Mr. Halsman is as thoughtful and wise as he is talented. During my interview with him about peoples' self-images, he spoke of feeling unattractive himself all of his life. He said that a famous actress had remarked the night before my interview, "Philippe, you are beautiful." He said he could not understand what she meant by this—and he was not (consciously) being modest or self-effacing. After my interview with him, I could understand very well what she meant. Here was another beautiful person—not only emotionally but physically as well—who had gone through his whole life thinking he was unattractive. He said his family had always teased him about his nose and he felt particularly sensitive about it. Being as objective as I could be, I thought Mr. Halsman appeared to have a small, perfectly attractive nose, rather than the large, ugly one apparently reflected in his parents' and siblings' eyes. But here he is, the world's greatest portrait photographer, with a beautiful, sensitive face himself—and a perfectly acceptable nose—and he feels he is unattractive! Another perfect example of a horizontal split and the retention of a negative self-image from his youth that certainly has no objective reality. If Mr. Halsman could continue to cling to his negative self-image without reason, I suppose it is not difficult to understand that others can do the same, sometimes with more objective reasons.

Mr. Halsman told me that when he takes a picture he attempts to penetrate the mask that people put on in dealing with the world, in order to get a portrait of the true person. Children up to the age of five or six or seven are not at all self-conscious in front of a camera; they act as if the camera is not even present. After that, they begin to be conscious of themselves and to worry about whether or not they are attractive. From then on, they try to pose—to present a mask that will be acceptable to the world, rather than to show who they really are. This would indicate that, by a certain age many of them have received enough negative reflections to make them feel unattractive as people. The English psychologist, D. W. Winnicott, made a distinction between the *real self* and the *false self*. By the false self, he meant the picture of ourselves that was acceptable to mother or other significant figures. Mr. Halsman makes the same distinction in portraiture. He says we try to hide the part of ourselves which we have had reflected as weak, ugly, or unacceptable, and present to the world a mask which conforms to what we were taught was acceptable.

Mr. Halsman says almost all the people he photographs are essentially interested in looking beautiful. Women almost universally want their pictures to look beautiful, rather than intelligent or thoughtful. Even women writers or comediennes want to be photographed in a way that makes them look beautiful, rather than funny or wise. Mr. Halsman could recall only one exception, a very stupid but lovely actress who wanted to be made to look intelligent. Men are a little less obsessed with looking beautiful; some seem, at times, to be more interested in looking wise or strong or showing they have character. This would indicate to me that few of us get as much positive reflection of our physical attractiveness as we require. So, for goodness sakes, if you feel that someone you care about looks good, don't hesitate to tell him. And don't be bashful about seeking compliments on how you look.

Of course, this also emphasizes that what we take into our self-esteem system is also very much a function of the culture in which we live. Our culture places enormous emphasis on physical attractiveness. Despite minor changes in the past ten years, it is a sexist culture that stresses physical attractiveness for women. It is only natural that what Mr. Halsman observes is a tremendous emphasis—especially in women—on beauty. What determines what we will value in ourselves is what is valued in societal culture and how this is passed on to us through the narrower culture of our nuclear family. There can be some variation of general cultural patterns if our particular parents are mavericks, but even then it is difficult for them to transcend their own cultural values, or for *us* to transcend them, even if our parents are in conflict with accepted beliefs.

As a rule, each person has a particular image of himself that he defines as how he really looks. This image comes first from looking in the mirror. Interestingly enough, says Mr. Halsman, when we look into the mirror we choose the angle and the pose that makes us look our best. We are usually, but not always, accurate observers and judges of our best features. Sometimes our ideas about ourselves and our images correspond to objective reality; sometimes they don't. Lyndon Johnson, for instance, would only allow photographs of his profile from the left side. Hubert Humphrey liked best the way he looked from the right side. Mr. Halsman was assigned to do a medal-type photograph of them for the cover of *Newsweek* when they were running for president and vice-president. Mr. Humphrey—who yielded to Mr. Johnson on more im-

portant issues than profiles—immediately realized that
he would have to yield to Mr. Johnson again and allow
the "wrong" side of his face to be shown in profile. I
asked Mr. Halsman whether there was a real difference
in the two sides of their faces morphologically. He replied that Mr. Johnson's profiles were, in fact, the
same from both sides, but that the president felt he
looked more noble from the left. In reality, Mr.
Humphrey's profiles were quite different and he was
correct in his belief that he looked much better from
the right side than the left.

Mr. Halsman tries to capture the most flattering
view of his subject, especially when the *subject* is com-
missioning the photograph because it is that person
who later judges the portrait. If he is commissioned by
a magazine or newspaper, he tries to take a photograph
that pleases *him*, not his subject. If his subject is paying for the portrait, then Mr. Halsman observes the
way the individual looks at himself in the mirror and
takes instant shots for an idea of what is thought to be
the most flattering image. He has never run across a
person who rejected a portrait because it was *too* flattering. Again, this is evidence that it must be extremely
rare for someone to get *too* much enhancement of his
physical self. Besides remembering and seeing themselves in a best photograph and a best angle in the mirror, older people display what Mr. Halsman calls "The
Phenomenon of the Lost Image." Apparently people
never have images of themselves past the forties or fifties. A seventy-year-old is invariably shocked at his
photograph, even after it has been retouched to take
off ten or fifteen years. Older people's self-image remains at fifty. People invariably say, "Am I really so
fat?" That is because we see in three dimensions, while
a photograph has only two; this adds 10 or 15 percent
to our weight in a photograph. That is why models
invariably must be ten or fifteen pounds underweight.

The more insecure a person is—the more self-
observing—the more he suffers from an inferiority
complex and is likely to present a mask. If a person is

secure, he will be more apt to feel natural. Mr. Halsman recalled that André Gide, the French writer, who appeared imperturbable, disintegrated completely in front of the camera. Apparently he was afraid of the impression he would make. Another man, perhaps one of the most beautiful men Mr. Halsman had ever photographed, was so insecure about his appearance he would never look into a mirror—even while shaving.

Security is clearly not a result of how beautiful a person actually is; it relates more to his *image* of himself. This is the distinction we make between the objective and the subjective view of ourselves. In line with this, Mr. Halsman has found that success or fame makes a big difference in the degree of anxiety of a subject while being photographed. On taking a second portrait of a noted author, Mr. Halsman observed that the writer appeared to be much more relaxed than the first time around. "Of course," was the answer. "My last book was a big success." Mr. Halsman has taken Johnny Carson's picture three times. At each succeeding sitting, Carson was more relaxed because of increasing success and inner security. This certainly confirms the idea that, even in adult life, great success and admiration can increase our self-esteem.

People are much less anxious in a group photograph than they are in a portrait. When I asked Mr. Halsman why, he said, "Well, wouldn't you be less scared if a man was pointing a revolver at a group in which you were standing, rather than at you alone?" I laughed and said that perhaps the choice of the metaphor of the camera as a revolver was not accidental. Agreeing, he said that an insecure person experiences the camera as piercing his mask and showing the world who he actually is. Halsman continued, "They think they are actually nothing—not worthy of being photographed. They usually feel secure because they know how to manipulate people. But you cannot flatter a camera. It is a glass eye. They feel observed, naked, exposed. They feel they can maintain control and handle a human being, but not a camera. They feel the camera will expose their weakness, whereas they have a mask that ordinarily covers it. All their lives they have been taught how to hide their feelings, how to be polite and charming and pleasing with people, but they don't know how to act in front of a camera."

Once again, this emphasizes the fact that so many of us have deficits in our self-esteem. We think we get by because we have learned to fool people so that they do not see who we really are. We feel that if they knew who we really were, they would reject us out of hand. The mask we put on for the world is to conceal our low self-image and to present an acceptable false self.

Women with beautiful bodies, who are sure of their beauty, will agree, sometimes surprisingly easily, to be photographed nude. Even though they have reputations as great and very proper ladies, they have amazingly few inhibitions as long as they feel their bodies are really beautiful. The pleasure in the positive reflection of their self-image overcomes their inhibitions. There is no great difference in photographing a famous person and an ordinary one. Famous people, Halsman feels, often have more interesting faces. However, there is a great difference between psychological and morphological photogeneity. Even people with beautiful or interesting faces can freeze up and become self-conscious in front of a camera. Their inner image of themselves does not correspond to their outer image. People, as with Mr. Halsman and his nose, have a tendency to retain reflected images of childhood. Apparently noses are frequent anatomical targets for ridicule. Here again we see the difference between objective reality and subjective reality—how our self-image, formed in childhood, may or may not be altered by our life experiences.

When a subject is facing the camera, Mr. Halsman tries to make him forget he is being photographed, for it is a very artificial situation. He talks to his subject, trying to establish a relationship. Sometimes he attempts to throw a subject off base, to strip the situation of its stiffness. For instance, he asked Mrs. Roosevelt whether she was interested in boxing. To his surprise, she said she was. He works to turn the artificial circumstance into a natural one. Sometimes he and his assistants even plan an "accident," in order to throw the subject off-guard and penetrate his frozen mask. Sometimes he tells a small joke. He could not get President Nixon to smile, so he told him a joke about a woman who asked the zoo keeper whether a hippopotamus was male or female. "That," said the zoo keeper, "should be of interest only to another hippopotamus." Nixon loved the joke and did not stop smiling for fifteen minutes. His false self had been penetrated.

Most people Mr. Halsman has photographed were very pleased with their portraits. This is no surprise, since he is a master at relaxing them, catching them off-guard, using lighting and camera angle to brilliant advantage, and also knowing from instant shots how they like to see themselves. However, there are exceptions. Vivian Leigh was so outraged by what Halsman thought were beautiful photographs of her that she tore up all of them into little pieces and said, "I will destroy you if you publish these in *Life* magazine." That night her husband, Sir Laurence Olivier, who had seen the contact prints of the pictures, called and said they were fine, that Halsman should go ahead and submit them. When Halsman met Vivian Leigh again three years later, she had apparently forgotten all about the incident, and was very cordial and friendly. Ingrid Bergman absolutely hated a picture of herself that Halsman and others thought was one of the loveliest ever taken of her. He had photographed her as happy, healthy, and wholesome. Twenty years later, he showed her the same photograph and she still hated it. Possibly her self-image was more sophisticated. Again we are faced with the difference between our image of ourselves and the reality of ourselves.

Henri Soulé, owner of the famous restaurant Pavilion, came from humble origins. He had never liked a picture of himself until Halsman took one. Soulé always felt he did not look as fine a gentleman as the people he served. Halsman caught him as sophisticated and intelligent, rather than reflecting the inner image he had of himself, of which he was ashamed.

In his introduction to *The Jump Book*, in which Halsman has caught many famous people in the act of jumping, he says that our face was given to us more to hide than to reveal our inner selves. We are taught to dissimulate, to conceal our negative feelings for people we don't like, to keep smiling, to keep a stiff upper lip. Our face seldom shows who or what we really are. Everybody wears armor. Everybody hides behind a mask. This mask had to be formed to ward off negative responses we received, or thought we received, to our real selves. Thus the masks are naturally even more exaggerated in front of a camera. Often we are interested in people because we want to see what is behind that mask. Romances, especially, are inclined to start and to persist in an attempt to pierce the loved one's enigmatic armor. Why is the Mona Lisa so fascinating? We hope that, in a cataclysm of passion, the mask will come off and we may be able to see the real person. Perhaps that is one reason why we are so excited by our ability to produce an orgasm in our partners. It is certainly a very important reason, in fact, why many people are unable to have an orgasm, or at best have a very controlled orgasm, in the presence of another person, whereas they might be able to have one during masturbation.

Halsman feels he has found a new psychological tool in analyzing the way people jump and the way they look while jumping. Apparently it is very difficult to maintain a mask while going against gravity, although some masks are held so tightly that nothing will loosen them.

Some people are conceited, with grandiose ideas about their own beauty, while some have diminished views of their own attractiveness. But most people's inner picture of themselves is streaked with their vulnerability. This must reflect the pain they have felt from assaults on their self-image. Halsman recounted a story of a young woman who thought of herself as having a thin, ugly body. He reassured her of her actual beauty and photographed her showing this. Despite her modesty, he got her to pose in the nude. The pictures turned out to be exceptionally beautiful. He met her by accident a year later, and she told him that the photographs had had an enormous impact on her life. She said that, up until the time he had taken the photographs, she felt so unattractive she had never allowed anyone to see her nude. The photographs had made such a difference in her self-image that she was now engaged to be married!

I wondered if there might be a new treatment called psychophotography. Perhaps some people, for whom there is a tremendous discrepancy between the negative images they have of their bodies and the reality, might be helped by seeing photographs of themselves that showed them in a more flattering light. I recalled to Halsman that I did not think I had ever met a woman who thought she had beautiful breasts. Some thought their breasts were too small, too large, or had ugly nipples. Halsman surprised me: "Actually, they are usually right," he said. "Very few women really have beautiful breasts. The trouble with using photographs to enhance someone's image is that you have to have an excellent photographer taking them. And even then they might not look good to the subject."

I still feel that photographs could be used constructively for many of the patients I see with poor body images. Nude photographs might be especially useful. Many of us have distorted images of parts of our body, images that do not usually show in ordinary photographs. Have you ever had a nude photograph taken of yourself? I haven't, and not very many people I know have—even in an era which allows male and female centerfolds. Perhaps nude photographs might counter some negative physical self-images.

At the end of the interview, which I had taped, Mrs. Halsman came in and asked if I had played any of it back. I said I had not. "Good," she said. "Philippe hates the way he sounds on tape." Another projection of a negative self-image. Mr. Halsman's voice is strong and steady. It reveals depth, warmth, intelligence, liveliness, and a fine sense of humor. Yet he is not alone. How many of us are actually shocked when we hear our voices on a tape recorder?

CHAPTER 14

Self-image and Sex

An important ramification of our self-image is the impact it has on our sexual lives. Self-image and sexuality are connected in a variety of strange ways. *Actual* physical attractiveness has little relationship to one's ability to enjoy sex. However, defects in our *image* of ourselves can have a profound effect on our sexual preferences, activities, and ability to enjoy ourselves. People who *feel* they are unattractive will tend to avoid making contacts with potential sexual partners. Philippe Halsman took nude photographs of a beautiful girl who felt she was ugly; by allowing her body to be viewed by a man for the first time in her life, she found that her photographs and their beauty had a profoundly positive effect upon her ability to engage in sex, owing to the effect on her self-image.

In my own practice, I have encountered many similar situations. One of my patients, Alice, was a very attractive woman with modest breasts. She felt so ashamed of her breasts, thinking them unusually small, that she was afraid to expose herself to a man. Participating in a group therapy marathon—a group therapy session that lasts for several hours—she was discussing her problem with the other members. Spontaneously, the group encouraged her to disrobe in front of them as a way of getting past her phobia. She was extremely reluctant to do so. Finally, as a way of inducing her to deal with her problem, all of the members of the group decided to disrobe. This was hardly an easy task for many of them, since they too had their own body-image problems. However, in the spirit of helping a friend, they managed to do so. Now, though still with a great deal of reluctance, Alice disrobed, except for re-moving her brassiere. With much passage of time and much encouragement she finally removed her brassiere and exposed her breasts. The group was honest in its response. Yes, her breasts were somewhat small, but by no means ugly, and the total picture she presented was a very attractive one. Alice could trust the group to be honest with her, since they had always been very frank about many aspects of her they did *not* like. The experience had a profound effect on her. In her fan-tasy, her breasts were so ugly that the men in the room would have run out in disgust. That was what she re-ally feared—that she would be mortified and humili-ated. When this did not occur, she was able to get past her phobia and began to have sexual relations with men.

About the same time, I was treating a male patient who was himself a therapist. He had the problem of feeling that his penis was small. He had not avoided sex entirely because of it, but he went around thinking that he had a bodily defect and was very reluctant to begin new sexual liaisons. He also felt uncomfortable about undressing in locker rooms in the presence of other men. Shortly after I had described to him my pa-tient's experience in the marathon group, he was in the midst of a marathon with his own patients. The discus-sion got around to problems of body image, and my patient very courageously told his group about his own problem. Not knowing what had happened in my group, his group had the same reaction. They suggest-ed that he and the other men in the group remove their clothing and that he compare the size of his penis with those of the other men. With some reluctance he did so. He reported to me that, in fact, his penis *was* the smallest of any of those in the group, but still the experience got him past his self-consciousness over the size of his penis. Even though his penis was the smallest, the difference in size was not much and no one responded to him in any negative way. The expected humiliation did not occur. After that he no longer felt uncomfortable, and shortly thereafter was even able to engage in nude bathing in a group, without anxiety. Interestingly enough, as we further analyzed his problem with his self-image, we discovered that he had incorporated into it the body of his father who had had a crippling disease. My patient's feeling that *he* had a deformed body was an internalization of the shame he had felt about his father's body.

This mechanism of our introjecting (taking into ourselves and making our own) negative feelings we have about the body of our parent of the same sex is, incidentally, another important explanation for distortions in our body image. I have a beautiful, slim, young patient who constantly sees herself as her fat, dumpy, sixty-year-old mother. This patient dressed and acted as if she really was built like her mother, going to all kinds of lengths to hide her body, until these connections were made conscious for her. If there is a gross disparity between your view of your body and the reality of it, as reflected by your friends and lovers, try to examine whether it is your mother or father's body that you have unconsciously put into your own. This mechanism—albeit an unusual, pathological one—is not uncommon.

From these two examples, as well as your own general internal and external experiences, I am sure you know that one of the major distortions people experience in their body image derives from feelings about external sexual organs. I used to say that almost every man I ever treated thought his penis was too small. On this score—and to point out the almost total lack of relevance to the degree of sexual enjoyment involved—in thirty years of practice I have had only two female patients ever complain about the size of a man's penis.

And to show that truth is often stranger than fiction, I found, to my surprise, that the lover they were complaining about turned out to be the same man! Even these two women did not reject this man as a lover, and both would have been delighted to marry him, if asked. So the reaction among men that their penis is not big enough is almost universal. (In fact, there are very rare situations in which this may actually be so. One friend of mine—a sexologist—advises that, if your penis measures more than four and a half inches when erect, it is a perfectly adequate size to perform satisfactorily sexually. If it is smaller than that, you should see an endocrinologist. Male sex hormones might be of value in increasing penis size.)

As many problems as men have about the size of their penises, women seem to have as many more about their breasts. Practically no woman I have ever met felt she had attractive breasts; in her view, they were either too small or too large, too pendulous or with unattractive nipples. Though women's negative view of themselves so often focuses on their breasts, at times the focus is on their hips or thighs or legs, or other parts of the body, too. Though I disagree with Freud's view that so-called penis envy is an inevitable consequence of being female, I do think that many women have problems about their body image that appear to have some roots in this issue. By "penis envy," Freud meant that every girl experiences the lack of a penis as a defect of her body. Because of this, she grows up feeling inferior to men, as if she has been damaged or deprived or is missing a part. I do not feel that this is a psychobiological imperative experienced by all women. On the other hand, I do feel that women who have been toilet-trained at too early an age, or in too severe a fashion, may have experienced their inability to establish urinary and anal control at the time that their mother expected it as due to a defective excretory apparatus. When these girls see that boys have penises, they conclude that the reason for their inability to control their bladder at the time expected by their mother was because of their lack of a penis. This leads them to feel that there is something wrong with their bodies. In addition, if they have brothers who are favored in the family, these girls may well feel that their lack of a penis is at the bottom (no pun intended) of the problem.

As psychoanalyst Clara Thompson pointed out in her paper in the early 1940s, and as many others have pointed out since, we do live in a definitely sexist culture that clearly favors men over women in many ways. Phallic worship is not uncommon in many primitive societies; phallic symbols are still used a great deal in art. So the roots of penis envy, in my mind, lie in the toilet-training issue and the preferential treatment of male children in the family—as well as in the culture at large—rather than in any psychobiological imperative. Nevertheless, many women in our society do grow up with the feeling that there is something wrong with their bodies. This feeling is frequently displaced from the genital to other areas of the body, especially more visible ones, such as the breasts. Aside from this displacement, few women in my experience have very positive feelings about their vaginas. This may reflect some results of the combination of toilet-training problems, male-sibling preference, and the sexist culture. So the tendency toward a negative body image, as frequently as it may occur among men, occurs much more frequently among women in our culture. Some women with very negative body images may become homosexual in order to avoid the invidious comparison, though I am not implying this is the only—or even the most important—reason for their choice.

"Fag hags"—women who are constantly in the company of homosexual men—are another example of women who may have severe problems with their body image. One interesting dynamic in the unconscious of women who tend to go out with homosexual men—with the conscious or unconscious intent of making them heterosexual—is the way they attempt to repair a defect in their own body image. Basically, these women

see themselves as defective men (without a penis).
They also see homosexual men as defective men. If
they can succeed in getting a homosexual man to have
sex with them (to repair *his* defective penis), they can
have more hope about the eventual repair of their own
bodily "defect."

What do we usually do with these feelings of ours
that revolve around not being *large* enough? Clearly,
we lionize men with large penises and women with
large breasts. Before the spread of the porno film in-
dustry, the lionization was restricted to women by both
sexes. Mae West, Jane Russell, Gina Lollobrigida, and
Sophia Loren represented externalizations and idealiza-
tions, for both men and women, of a wish to have large
external sexual organs. Now that we have porno flicks,
Big John Holmes and Harry Reems have become male
stars. Just as men and women like to look at women
with large breasts, both men and women like to see
men with large penises. In pre-Castro Cuba, "Super-
man," a Cuban with a twelve-inch penis who appeared
in sexual exhibitions, was one of the major tourist at-
tractions. Men who like movies of other men with large
penises are not necessarily homosexual. They may just
want to repair a defect in their view of their own geni-
tals by incorporating a large penis with their eyes and
identifying with the man who possesses it. Among ef-
feminate male homosexuals, there are so-called "size-
queens" who are drawn especially, and perhaps only,
to men with large penises. This is an excellent example
of an attempt to repair a wound in their body image, as
well as in their gender identity.

Of course, "too small" is not the only form of negative body image; "too large" can also be a defect. This
applies commonly to noses (witness Mr. Halsman),
but can also apply to breasts, thighs, tallness in wom-
en, ears, feet, and other body parts.

I have already observed how men's interest in
voyeurism is an attempt to derive vicarious satisfaction
from unconsciously identifying with a person with a

beautiful body who is free to display it to get admiration and adulation.

In fact, the beauty of our body and the size of our external sexual organs need very rarely affect our ability to enjoy sex. Unfortunately for many of us, our images of our bodies are so negatively distorted that we may feel humiliated about displaying them. This, of course, can have a marked effect, not only on our finding partners but on our ability to enjoy sex when we have found them. It can also influence our choice of partners, leading us to pick mates on the basis of narcissistic extension, as we have discussed in a previous chapter. It can direct us toward beautiful people, or even toward people with large external sexual organs, who may not be the right sexual partners or good for us in any other way. There are many ways that a negative body image, especially about our sexual organs, can inhibit us and put a damper on our enjoyment.

Masters and Johnson and others in the field of sexual therapy spend a great deal of time helping people with sexual dysfunctions to look in the mirror, to learn to love and appreciate their bodies, to learn to take pleasure from their bodies through masturbation or through the caresses from their partners. A healthy love of one's own body is essential for an optimum sex life, as well as for a general feeling of self-esteem.

Neither our body image nor our sexual self-image is permanently fixed. Hopefully, they can be changed by this book and other educational measures. If more is needed, there are psychotherapists who focus on changing our image of our body by such measures as the Alexander method (which works on body tensions), dance therapy, bioenergetic therapy, and others. If still more is required, sexual therapy can be helpful, and, of course, psychoanalysts like myself are available to assist you to get at the deepest unconscious roots of these problems.

It needs to be stated that our body image is not the only part of our total self-image that affects our view of ourselves as sexual people, and eventually our ability to enjoy sex and to give sexual enjoyment. Sex is obviously connected with much more of our self-image than just our view of our body. There are very handsome men and very beautiful women whose self-images, as far as their bodies go, are realistic, since they do feel beautiful. Yet some of these people may feel very inadequate about their sexuality and may, in fact, suffer from sexual dysfunctions such as impotence, inability to have orgasms, and other problems.

I have a patient who is a movie star, and very much aware of his exceptional good looks. But he is also aware of his inability to get really close to another person. He has never been able to experience the feeling of being in love. He knows he is lacking in the ability to care deeply for another human being. Though conscious that he is physically attractive and that he can perform well, if mechanically, during sex, his total self-image as a sexual man is quite low since he realizes his emotional poverty. One can enjoy sex without love, but the ability to love and to be loved certainly enhances one's sexual enjoyment. And the inability to be emotionally intimate can have a marked effect on one's ability to find partners, as well as to enjoy sex with them.

The same kind of low sexual self-image can be experienced by an attractive person who feels lacking in charm or intelligence or personality. I have an exceptionally beautiful female patient who is aware of her beauty but keenly feels a lack in her ability to communicate with a man and engage him in conversation. She is awkward at a party or across a dinner table from a man. Despite her acknowledgment of her attractiveness, her total image of herself as a sexual woman is still lacking. And, obviously, a person who is ignorant about sex, and inexperienced, will likely feel insecure about himself or herself in bed.

As I have said our total image of ourselves as sexual people is not necessarily fixed. Since our sexual self-image is based on our body image and on our image as total people able to communicate, be emotionally intimate, love and be loved, as well as on our specific knowledge about sex, there are many available ways for us to increase our sexual self-image. These means of developing ourselves include sex education, social clubs and groups, schools, courses, how-to books and lessons, and all forms of therapy, including psychoanalysis. In the next chapter, there is an interview with Monica Kennedy, America's foremost strip-teaser, obviously a symbol of sexuality. We will see that her sexual attractiveness is based on much more than a good body, or her good feeling about her good body.

CHAPTER 15

An Interview with Monica Kennedy, America's Foremost "Strip-teaser"

For those of you who are not aficionados of burlesque and may not have heard of her, Monica Kennedy has had a reputation as the country's foremost strip-teaser for at least a decade. Today, strip-teasing is not what it used to be. Even a performer like Monica is more of an entertainer than a stripper, but she does perform in the nude, after taking off her clothes, and performs some rather explicit—and, to some people, rather shocking—sex acts.

I thought an interview with Monica might shed some light on some of the issues we are confronting here—narcissism, exhibitionism, grandiosity, and others. Monica is a woman "d'un certain âge"—in other words, it is difficult to judge her age, but I would guess she is in her middle to late thirties. Her body is ample; some would call her heavy, especially from the waist down. She has a very attractive face—child-like but with an intelligent gaze—and a perpetual smile that is real rather than forced. She is very open emotionally. One makes contact with her instantly; there are no walls, no barriers. She loved being interviewed and proved to be a non-stop talker. It was only with effort that I was able to introduce the specific questions I had prepared. She is charming, friendly, and lovable. She exudes not a drop of meanness or conceit, despite her very high opinion of herself and an almost boundless enthusiasm for talking about herself, for exposing herself physically, mentally, and spiritually. She told me first about the long accounts of her in Earl Wilson's book, *Show Business Laid Bare,* as well as in *Cheri* magazine. She was obviously delighted at any attention paid to her, whether by writers like myself, men in an audience, or her lovers. In addition to her sex act, she writes music, sings, and is beginning to paint. Clearly, she is tremendously involved in getting and taking in attention and is able to do so in a completely unself-conscious way, without guilt, shame, or inhibitions.

When I asked her how she felt about her body, she said she felt great about it, except occasionally when she put on a little too much weight. Many women of comparable weight would feel very negatively about their bodies; she may be twenty or thirty pounds too heavy.

Monica said, "I love food and I love to go on food binges. I have to live for my public and look good, but I have to live for myself, too. Sometimes I'm a little overweight, but I think my body is beautiful."

I asked if there were any particular part of her body that she did not like, and she said no.

When she was young, she was uncomfortable with her sexuality because she had been raised in a strict, Catholic household, but she always knew her body was beautiful.

"Men used to walk into walls looking at my derriere. Now I'm not ashamed of my sexiness. God wants us to be happy, feel good, be in love, have lovers. I make my customers feel good. I make men happy. Women shouldn't put men down or make them think they're degenerate. If a man wants to try something, a woman should go ahead and let him, without putting him down. I'm married and I have two girls, nine and ten. I think I'm an extraordinary woman 'cause I keep lots of men happy. My husband doesn't mind sharing me with other men. I can keep my husband, my kids, and my fans happy and still have time to write music and make records as a singer."

I asked her if she spent much time in front of a mirror. She said she didn't; she just doesn't have the time. In my opinion, she is really *not* self-centered. She does not need to be. She feels the men in her audience love her and she loves them. As a man frequently in her audience, I can certainly vouch for this.

She says, "I feel a lot of affection for them and they do for me. After all, I've grown up with them. I feel married to them. They're my friends. The only ones I feel a little bad for are some of the doctors and lawyers and politicians. Some of them feel a little funny about what I do in my act now. I really go the limit. I don't like to embarrass them. I know they loved me when I was much straighter and I don't want them to feel funny. Be sure to put that down in your book. I really feel bad about *their* feeling uncomfortable. They say, 'You know, I come here to see you, Monica, but I don't really like this place or what you do.' "

I asked her if she ever felt uncomfortable doing her act in front of women. She said she didn't—that she feels she is teaching them something.

She was born on a 100-acre farm in Virginia and was the oldest of eight children. Farm life taught her to be very self-sufficient, able to get along without electricity or a telephone. She had to take care of the younger children, which might have added to her grandiosity by giving her responsibilities greater than a child usually has at that age. Her mother gave her enough attention, but her father, an alcoholic, did not. She was a virgin when she got married. Now she has a lot of sexual fantasies, in addition to doing her sex act, being a wife, and having lovers.

"My husband and my lovers are jealous of my sexual fantasies. They'll probably give me a hard time even if they read in your book that I have them."

I offered not to mention them.

"Oh no," she said, as exhibitionistic as ever, "I *want*

you to put that in your book even if it will get me in trouble with them."

This was an excellent example of Monica's seeking attention and loving to expose her psyche in order to get it, even if it resulted in some negative consequences. She was willing to risk disapproval by exposing herself in a way that might get her attention.

I asked her if she had any problems. She said her only problem was to keep up with two houses, two children, a husband, her fans, singing, and writing music. She needs time to herself. She is always "stretched out too far." I suggested that perhaps being the oldest of eight children had created in her a feeling of responsibility. Obviously, she saw being able to accomplish all these tasks as pulling off an impossible stunt.

She says, "I'm a sort of superwoman."

I was struck here by her open admission of grandiosity; *her* grandiosity is not at all hidden in any closet. This became even more evident when I asked her if she had any fears of growing old.

She answered very candidly. "I know I can never get old if I don't want to, because getting old comes from your thoughts. I don't worry about wrinkles. You can't get a wrinkle if you don't allow it."

Again I was struck by her hidden feeling of immortality and total control over her aging process.

I asked, "Well, what about if you're eighty years old?"

She said, "Even if you are eighty, you don't have to look eighty. What makes you old is your nutrition and your thoughts. Power comes from Christ. I am one-half of him. I believe I have Christ in me. We all have great power and control. Most of us don't develop our spirit enough. I can stay young as long as I keep my spirit. I'm actually three people in one—a homebody, a sexpot, and an intellectual. I'm very educational. Earl Wilson said I'm the most educational woman he's ever talked to. I'm into psychology, too. I can function better with sex if I can get into a man's mind. I have to get into a person's mind and emotions to get him to enjoy sex. I have to be smart and listen to what they want. I know I have a lot of mystery about me. I know something that most people don't understand. I understand about life in a way that is different from the way other people do."

In this sequence Monica directly reveals her grandiose feelings about her beauty, accomplishments, spirit, wisdom, intellect, and even her ability to control her aging processes. In contrast to most of us, she has no fear or shame or discomfort about these feelings. She feels special, she wants attention, and she gets it.

I asked Monica if she takes in easily the love and admiration she gets. I was wondering if she had a vertical split (a disowning of the person who sought and received the admiration and an inability to take it in), so I asked if she ever felt uncomfortable about taking in praise. She said she takes in all the admiration she gets very easily and never feels conceited or worried about liking herself too much. In truth, despite all her clearly grandiose statements, she never struck me as a woman who was vain or self-centered. Her attention-getting seems natural, rather than compulsive. She said she always feels exactly like herself and never puts on an act or a false front for people, even on the stage, unless she is specifically and consciously playing a role. She loves her real self and has no need for a mask. She feels completely comfortable being Monica. Several times she told me to be sure to put something she had said in my book. She sought attention openly from me and from my readers. When she is performing, she says she feels very sensually turned on by her body. Her body image and her love of her body are certainly different from the images most of us have about our bodies. Her nipples often become erect because of her sensuality. She is also turned on by men's faces and their admiration. Some are shy; some are very aroused; some are masturbating. Rather than taking offense when her fans masturbate, it excites her and she is happy that she can stimulate them.

"You're up there to satisfy the fantasies of the men and yourself. I really enjoy it. I miss the stage-door Johnnies who would bring me flowers and gifts and write letters to make secret, romantic dates with me. Sex is more exciting if it's more romantic. A woman is sexier if she is wearing something—even a chain around her waist—than when she is totally nude. It leaves more to the imagination. I think women should always dress in skirts, not pants, with black stockings and a skirt slit halfway up the legs."

Here Monica was talking about her delight in being exhibitionistic and getting attention and admiration in that way. I asked her if there were any personality characteristics she has noticed about strippers.

"They're more outgoing, not phoney. They tell you how they feel. You know where they're coming from."

I suggested that they "let it all hang out—not just physically but also emotionally." She agreed that their minds are as stripped as their bodies. In this respect, they are quite different from most actors, who are known for their phoniness. She said some strippers worry about the way people feel about them; they worry that people will look down on them. They're sensitive; they like, or even love, what they're doing, but they don't like to be judged. Monica said she never feels judged or humiliated or mortified. However, she said four or five times that she was a little concerned about how her straighter, more sophisticated admirers—politicians and doctors and lawyers—might react to her cruder, more explicit sexual acts. Despite this, I felt that she was really more concerned about embarrassing *them* than she was about any humiliation to herself. So it seems that Monica does not have the problems about humiliation that most of us do.

She ended by saying she feels she is beautiful spiritually, from the inside. How she feels about herself depends more on how she feels from the inside than on whether her hair is exactly right. Again, she is not self-centered. She considers she gets her spirit from the Almighty, so she is usually buoyant and happy.

It is no wonder that Monica Kennedy is the country's number-one stripper. She embodies every man's open projection of his grandiose self. She feels that she is beautiful inwardly and outwardly, that she is a superwoman, that she is intellectual, that she has some secret, mysterious knowledge about the universe. She has no problem at all in seeking out admiration and no problem in taking it in. She has no fears about her grandiosity getting out of control. She feels loved by her fans and she loves them back. She exemplifies a person with a high level of self-esteem about her body, her mind, and her soul. She willingly and happily displays all of herself for others to look at, listen to, and admire. Her audience is almost universally appreciative of all her talents; she gets a tremendous amount of admiration and applause—literal and figurative. She feels no reluctance or shame about seeking approval. She is never hurt or humiliated by negative reactions to her. She easily and gracefully takes in all the admiration she gets, so her self-esteem is constantly growing. She exudes a feeling of self-love in a way that does not make her seem vain or self-centered. In short, she is the perfect extension for poor fellows like me, who have problems with our own self-image and our ability to display ourselves for admiration. And she is by far my favorite burlesque performer. Before I interviewed her, I knew I *felt* this, but I had no understanding of the reasons behind it. Now the reasons are eminently clear.

CHAPTER 16

Self-esteem—the Major Motivation for Our Actions

When I was a college sophomore, one of the more frequent philosophical debates I had with my roommate was whether there was such a thing as a truly altruistic act. If someone did something that appeared to be totally self-sacrificing—even giving up his life to save his friend's life—wasn't it really because there was some kind of pleasure or personal gain in it for him? This debate was an old chestnut that could be roasted eternally. There appeared to be no clear answer. One could take either side of the question and argue quite effectively for it. So why am I raising this same question, almost forty years later? The reason is that for the first time in my life, and since the new psychoanalytic understanding of narcissism, I think that there is a definitive answer to it. Until now, I think that even psychoanalytic theory was embroiled in a mistaken view of the major motivation for our actions.

Freud very clearly focused on our so-called instincts as the primal driving force that motivates us. He, of course, focused his theories on our sexual instincts. It certainly is a fact that men have androgens and women have estrogens—that is, hormones produced by our bodies that work eventually on our brains and push us in the direction of gratifying our sexual impulses. Freud felt that the basis of neurosis was the inhibition of the gratification of these impulses. His original theory was *very* simplistic and biological. Anxiety arose from the damming up of sexual impulses. He even placed the blame specifically on coitus interruptus. This was the practice, common in the late nineteenth century in Vienna, of the man withdrawing his penis from the vagina and ejaculating externally, in order to prevent conception. Freud felt that the emotional frustration in this act was so great as to bring about tremendous difficulties, a damming up of sexual energy (which he called libido), and the appearance of anxiety and other neurotic problems.

Freud did not remain content very long with this theory as a basic explanation, modifying it after a few years. However, despite his de-emphasis, the idea persisted, indeed still persists even in sophisticated analytic circles, that what motivates a person in the main are his biological drives and what causes his problems is a frustration in his ability to gratify these drives. I am not suggesting that this idea is *totally* erroneous, but I believe it is less important than it has been thought to be, and is not central.

A later psychoanalytic development, propounded especially by English psychoanalysts such as Melanie Klein, R. W. D. Fairbairn, D. W. Winnicott, and Henry Guntrip, focused attention away from the idea of gratification of instincts and toward the need that *people* have for other *people*. In this frame of reference, the cause of unhappiness is our inability to achieve the closeness with other people we require; the problem lies in those aspects of ourselves that prevent human closeness. *Drive gratification* (as in Freud) is replaced by *need for personal contact* and closeness. Attention is focused on people's fear of rejection or abandonment or engulfment by another person, growing usually out of traumatic experiences in childhood. Expecting the same early experiences to be repeated in later contacts with people, we avoid opportunities for closeness or, at the very least, limit them. To the meagerness in the quantity or quality of contact is ascribed the cause of most of our unhappiness. This point of view certainly has a great deal of merit and in many ways seems closer to our personal emotional experience than the Freudian theory. We are more apt to *feel* "I need someone" than "I need sexual gratification." To me, this point of view also has some limitations in explaining *all* of human behavior. While I believe it accounts for a great deal, I still think there is a missing link that can now be supplied by a greater understanding of our self-esteem system.

What I am really saying is that, to a great extent, our behavior is motivated not only by our need for instinctual gratification or our need for closeness with other people but also by our need to maintain our own self-esteem. Why am I sitting here, writing this book this Saturday morning, after working very hard all week and being truly tired? I am not getting any sexual or any other instinctual gratification out of it. And I am not getting closer to anyone else in the process of doing it, nor am I likely to after publication. As a matter of fact, my wife is somewhat annoyed that I am excluding her from contact with me. The act of writing may well produce present and future estrangement between us.

So what is pushing me on? Surely it is that I will think more of *myself*—I will give myself points—for writing this book. I may or may not get many points from the outside—perhaps some. But still, why do I make this particular choice at this moment? In terms of myself, I have an explanation that clarifies why *I* write books and other people don't. When I was a small child, even an infant, I was pretty much given by my mother into my grandfather's care. He took care of me, toilet-trained me and basically motivated me. He was the second son of a family in a small town in Italy with the means to send only one son to college. So his older brother went to college, and proceeded to squander the family's money, never getting an education. My grandfather, frustrated in his longing for an education, had to become a tailor, instead of the professional he so wanted to be. Eventually he came to America and encouraged both his sons to become professionals, which they did. When I was handed over to him, he decided—consciously or unconsciously—that I would live out for him his frustrated dream of becoming a truly world-famous intellectual.

With this in mind, he had me reading and writing by the time I was three. When I went to kindergarten at age five, I had been so indoctrinated by him in the value of learning that I refused to stay in kindergarten. "These children spend all day long playing," I said. "I did not come to school to play. I came here to study and learn." In many ways, this story seems one of the most pathetic ones I have ever heard. Here I was, a five-year-old child, already so conditioned that I could not enjoy play. Nevertheless, I made such a fuss that the school actually put me in the first grade. So my self-esteem system had been formed by then. I gave *myself* credit for working and demerits for play. Here I am, fifty years later, still working and not playing. This does not gratify my biological instincts, and certainly not my sexual ones. Nor does it bring me closer to anyone. But still I do it—*because* it *makes me feel good.* Given my personal self-esteem system, I get more gratification from this than I would from making love or watching television or talking to my wife or children.

I have gone into this personal example at some length because I want to explain that it is our conditioning—in terms of what adds or detracts from our self-esteem—that is a stronger motivation for us than sex, love from *another* person, or even self-preservation. We can literally die to save another person because, by doing this, we think more highly of ourselves than we would by saving ourselves. A priest can get more satisfaction through renouncing sex than he would through a sexual experience, if his self-esteem system has been conditioned in that way. Subjecting ourselves to pain can be more gratifying (as with some masochists) than avoiding it. All of a sudden, if we take conditioning and the development of our self-esteem systems into account, some aspects of human behavior that have puzzled us begin to make sense.

This theory also explains the differences between people, and even the differences between people from different countries or regions. A person's behavior is very much determined by the values with which he has been inculcated, and that make him look good in his own eyes. These values are transmitted through the different systems of which he is a part—his nuclear family, his extended family, his community, his religious affiliations, his organizations, and all the other institutions of his particular society. How we are conditioned to act to add to our self-esteem is what characterizes us as unique and different from everyone else in the world. Whatever it is that has high value in our particular family or our especial culture is part of what we must value in ourselves. It is no use for our self-love to be tall if short is what is valued.

What keeps the whole process going and gives it such primacy in our eyes is our self-esteem. Even if we get past "caring what other people think"—in the negative sense of that expression—we certainly can never get past, nor would we want to, caring what we think of ourselves. This constant self-evaluating process, referred to in psychoanalysis as our *ego-ideal*, and our attempts to live up to it constitute, in my mind, a much greater factor in our motivation than our instincts or our need for *other* people's love and approval.

This self-esteem, or our own personal ego-ideal, forms the main bulwark of our uniqueness and our sense of ourselves. One of the psychoanalysts who split off from Freud, Alfred Adler, was probably on the right track when he focused his attention on the importance in human motivation of a drive for power and a need to compensate for a feeling of inferiority. However, at the time of his work the psychoanalytic ideas about narcissism had hardly even begun to evolve. So, though his work now makes a great deal of sense, his view was necessarily simplistic because of the lack of a strong conceptual and theoretical base. Now, more than fifty years later, we analysts are beginning to rediscover some of Adler's ideas, even while putting them in a somewhat different framework.

CHAPTER 17

Appropriate Ways of Enhancing Our Self-esteem

By now, we are aware (or should be) that we all need to love ourselves, to be "our own true love"—the person we love the best and the most. We know that this is a normal, healthy state of affairs and not anything for which we should feel shame. In fact, we know that if we do not love ourselves in this way we will be forced into many unhealthy, self-destructive situations. We may become self-centered—preoccupied with our appearance or our health or our finances or our success. We will be subject to serious mood swings that can result in self-loathing, depression, and even self-destruction. We will be very sensitive to slights, easily humiliated. We will not be able to weather the inevitable ill fortune from outside causes—accidents of nature, illness, loss, and other unexpected and "unfair" reversals. We will be unforgiving and cruel to ourselves when we do make mistakes that result in trouble. We will be afraid to take chances and compete to the best of our ability. We will be unable to enjoy fully our successes and our triumphs, and to take in the deserved praise and admiration we receive. We will tend to try to achieve the sense of feeling good about ourselves by connecting with other people who may possess what we feel or to whom we falsely attribute such qualities. This will make a mockery of our intimate relationships. Instead of choosing partners or friends because of their warmth and ability to communicate, we will be compelled to pick them for other qualities, real or fancied, that we ascribe to them. Projecting our possibly hidden sense of grandeur upon others, we will be disappointed in our relationships because we expect the impossible.

At this point, hopefully, we will have gotten past some of our fear and shame about our grandiose fantasies and our need to keep them hidden. Now we no longer require our horizontal or vertical splits to protect us from the imaginary dangers of allowing them into the open. We will no longer need to push down our self-esteem, or push away from us and disown admiration we get for our accomplishments. We have decided not to try to fill the gaps in our self-image through narcissistic extensions.

If we have cleared away some of our inner fears that have subdued our self-esteem, what can we do *externally* to help change things? Actually, there are a number of choices. First of all, we should try to make an accurate assessment of our assets. What do we really have that can bring us the admiration we need to raise our level of self-esteem? Do we, in fact, have a beautiful face or body, an extraordinary intellect, a good deal of money or power, a particular artistic or scientific talent? Hopefully, we can now assess ourselves without undue modesty. I advise people to rate themselves on a scale of one to a hundred in different departments. For example, Face–74, Body–77, Brains–92, Graphic art–31, Sense of humor–78, Music–22, Lover–78, Sensitivity–79, Organizing ability–88, Mechanical dexterity –27, Physical strength–68, Reliability–93, Flexibility–52, Ability to communicate–91, Sense of rhythm–46, Ability in sports–72, Cooking–31, Housekeeping–28, Writing–89, Mathematics–78, Natural sciences–75, Politics–82, Leadership–90, Taste in clothes and art–89, etc. Then we can judge our strong points that we can parlay into the attention-getting and admiration we need. There is no point in trying to get it for our singing if we can't carry a tune. We should concentrate our efforts at getting admiration by exhibiting those features, aspects and abilities that can earn it.

It is also important to realize that, although any admiration is welcome, we may have a particular need to be admired for certain qualities more than others. If we know we are very beautiful and also *feel* we are, we may not need to have this particular quality praised as much as another. People are very interesting in their choices of qualities they need to have praised. We have already pointed out the fact that the value to us of qualities is determined by our general culture, our particular subculture, and, more specifically, the various systems in which we function—our nuclear family, our extended family, our school, our religion, our community, etc.

In addition to these determinants, Alfred Adler expounded a theory of "compensation for organ inferiority" that has made a great deal of sense to me in the course of my clinical experience. When people have a *real*—not imagined or subjective—deficit, they usually have a tendency to deny it and overcompensate for it. If they have any feelings of inadequacy or unacceptability about these real organic defects, they tend to overlook them, suppress them, and perhaps displace them onto other parts of themselves. Once I had a patient who had a withered left arm as a result of a birth injury. When she bemoaned her lack of success with men, she never attributed it to her real defect. Rather, she felt that her nose was unattractive and she considered having plastic surgery. In fact, her nose was almost perfect. I had another patient who was quite unattractive physically, but brilliant intellectually. He never complained about his lack of good looks, but perceived himself as stupid. Yet another patient was a very successful photographers' model, extraordinarily beautiful but not especially intelligent. She had all sorts of pretensions about being an intellectual, but was constantly berating herself because of her lack of attractiveness. A blind patient objected strongly to my use of the word "blind" and insisted I refer to his disability as "sightless." Mentally retarded people are rarely disturbed about their intellectual inferiority; they tend to deny it.

The point of all these examples is that if you have a *real* deficit in yourself that is not very amenable to change, the chances are that you will deal with it and not seek praise for it. You will probably deny it and automatically attempt to compensate for it by trying to excel in some other area. Or you may make up for it with a narcissistic extension, as in the example of the short man who goes out with tall women. You will not seek to receive admiration for something you lack that truly could not or would not be admired. Very likely, you would dismiss it as unimportant. For instance, I rate very low in manual dexterity. I like to joke about the fact that I have difficulty screwing in a light bulb. I reduce my failing to insignificance and, therefore, am not bothered by it. However, in the past I was terribly bothered by my intellectual lacks, despite consistent high standings in my classes and other evidence to the contrary.

The areas in which we want to be and need to be admired are regularly the areas in which there is a great disparity between our subjective view of ourselves and the reality. I have little need for admiration of my manual skills and, on those rare occasions in which I have received it, I have not gotten much of a rise in my self-esteem. On the other hand, I am constantly seeking admiration of my intellect (by teaching, by publishing professional articles, by writing this book, by lecturing). After seven books, I should have some security about my intellect, but I still seek and take in more and more admiration for it and my self-esteem continues to grow in this area. So, after your objective evaluation of yourself, you might think you would want to seek praise for some quality you do not really possess and that your search would be fruitless and frustrating. The opposite is true. You will need admiration for those qualities which you *do* possess, but for which, in the course of your life, you have neither received nor been able to take in praise. This is a fortunate circumstance, since you will probably deny the fact or the importance of real lacks, whereas you will try to get praise for qualities that you really *do* possess, even though you may not *subjectively feel* good about yourself in those areas.

Most important is that we recognize that our need for attention is not only normal but that its satisfaction is central to our well-being and will help enhance our self-esteem. This will make us feel good about ourselves, so we will not need to be so self-centered, but more self-loving. We will then be able to focus more *off* ourselves and *on* people and things around us.

After deciding what we have that will command admiration, we have to be very careful about picking our audience. We do not have to have a group of yes-men or worshipers, but we do have to choose people who really appreciate our particular qualities. There is no point in singing to a person who hates music. The one we pick must be generally responsive, and he must also be particularly responsive to the specific things we have to offer. Beyond that, he must be a person able to express his appreciation in a discernible manner—verbally, nonverbally, or both. There are many people around who may genuinely admire and respect us, but if they are unable to give praise or express positive feelings their inner reaction does us no good. How often have you heard from your mother, "Oh, your father is so proud of you. When he's with other people, he can't stop telling them about your accomplishments." You say, "But he never says a thing when *I'm* there." So Dad's pride in you doesn't do *you* any good. He is doing his bit of "child-wearing," getting an ego trip for *himself* from you. He isn't giving *you* anything. Such people are ungenerous. If you are going to seek praise and recognition, there is no point in trying to wrest it from them.

It is strange how people seem drawn to those who are withholding of praise and admiration—the very thing needed most. I wonder whether part of the attraction for us of these "withholders" may be that they never threaten our fear or shame about our grandiosity—since they never feed into it. They never praise us, so our hidden grandiosity remains untouched. I am sure this is not the only reason we are drawn to them. For instance, we can prove how powerful we are if we can manage to get blood out of one of these stones. But it is really important not to waste our attempts to get admiration on people who withhold it consistently. You can judge who is likely to appreciate your qualities, and also who is likely to be generous enough to let you know about it. If you yourself have trouble asking for praise, probably you will also have trouble giving it. As you open up your own capacity to seek out praise, you will also increase your ability to give it.

For many of you, it wouldn't do any good even to hire three Magi to follow you. You would still not be able to take in any admiration. Unless you go through the process of getting in touch with your grandiose fantasies and not needing to defend against them, any praise you get may not be incorporated into your self-esteem system. Beyond this—and this is *most* important—gratuitous praise, praise that is not specifically and consciously sought after, cannot be taken in well, not in the same way that sought-after praise is let into the self-esteem system. You have to seek it in order really to savor it. Taking in praise is not a passive process. You can't just sit there, with your ears and eyes open, and let it in. Rather, it is a very *active* process that involves the whole sequence of 1. being conscious of needing and seeking praise, 2. picking the particular quality that you will use to get it, 3. picking the person who will truly appreciate that quality and who can openly express his appreciation, and 4. taking in the praise. It is a complicated sequence that must be followed from beginning to end. Each one of the four steps must be followed in order for the praise to be able to get into your self-esteem system and help you to feel good about yourself. Even if you have cleared up your problem about being afraid or ashamed of your grandiosity, you haven't won the ball game yet. That is only the preparation, the preliminary—not the end result.

Let us take an example. You feel a bit down about yourself. You decide that you need some kind of admiration. You decide that you want to get it by having some friends over to dinner. You pick that method because you know you are a particularly fine cook and your cooking invariably gets you admiration. Now you have to decide on your guests. You choose friends who are gourmets and who really appreciate good cooking, but they must also be people whom you know are able to express their genuine appreciation to you, openly and directly. They arrive, are delighted by your meal, and give you a great deal of praise. You can take it in because you've acknowledged you needed it, you sought it consciously, and you found an appreciative and expressive audience.

I remember an experience with a woman whom I loved very much. She came over and spent an afternoon with me. I was very much in love with her and lavish in my praise of her beauty, her intelligence, and her character. We spent what seemed to be a lovely few hours together; I was very affectionate to her, both physically and verbally. Not long after she left, she telephoned me, saying she did not really understand why, but she did not feel satisfied. Something was missing. I told her I was delighted at the opportunity of seeing her again and asked her to come over that evening. When we were together she told me that she had felt very much in need of affection and praise during the afternoon, but that she had never acknowledged or communicated it to me. Even though she had gotten what she wanted, she had not gone through the process of admitting her need for praise or asking for it. She had worked out well two of the other three steps. She had picked the qualities she wanted praised—her physical and emotional self. She had chosen the person, me, who truly appreciated her qualities and could openly express his appreciation of her. But since she had left out step one—her conscious admission of needing praise and consciously seeking it out—she could not complete step four, taking in the praise which was offered. In effect, she had been to a banquet and had gone home starving because she had not acknowledged that she was hungry. Her subjective experience in the evening was totally different from her experience that afternoon. Her telephone call to me was an acknowledgment of her need. She received the same amount of praise from me for the same qualities, but this time she was able to take it in. The whole process was an active, conscious one on her part, while she was merely a passive recipient in the afternoon. She had gone away empty in the afternoon but was filled in the evening, despite the fact that I was exactly the same at both meetings and in *my* subjective experience there was no particular difference between them.

It is very important to remember that there is a whole process involved in taking in praise that is not too different from the process of taking in food. You must feel and acknowledge a hunger, know specifically what you want to eat, find a place where you can get it, and then ingest it and digest it. Gratuitous praise that is not sought after is fine, but it is not nourishing to your self-esteem system in the same way as consciously sought-after praise.

Let us take another example. I know that I need a great deal of praise and admiration. Let us say that I was invited to speak at a psychiatric meeting on the Psychology of the Self (as I have been). This is a subject in which I am very interested and to which I have given much thought and made some contributions. The conference was to be held in a distant city. My first impulse was to turn down the invitation; it would involve a considerable expenditure of time and money on my part. When I reconsidered my decision, I realized that I wanted and needed the admiration and professional recognition that my address would bring me. It would raise my level of self-esteem, would make me feel important. I have the expertise to present the paper, and my audience would consist of professionals likely to appreciate my contribution. I would certainly receive applause, admiration, and recognition for my effort. Having gone through this process, despite my initial impulse to refuse, there is no way now that I could possibly turn it down. Before the days of my ability to acknowledge my grandiose fantasies, to stop defending against them by a horizontal split, and thinking that I was not worthy of such an honor, I would surely have turned down this opportunity for an experience that would certainly add to my self-esteem and help buttress me against future failures, mistakes, and misfortunes.

It is an interesting paradox that the way to enhance your love for yourself involves opening yourself up to receiving admiration from others. In this sense, there is a quality of "bringing yourself up all over again" to the process of repairing the damage to your self-esteem. It is also a paradox that—once you have developed a sufficient quantum of self-esteem—you will be less dependent on the quality of the responses others give you, less sensitive to slights, and less easily humiliated or hurt or embarrassed.

What will happen when, hesitatingly, you first try this system of acknowledging your need and seeking out praise? First of all, you will have to recognize how high your resistance will be to doing this at all. You're going to be scared to death in the beginning. You'll be afraid of being discovered and laughed at, made fun of and humiliated for actively going after praise. You'll just have to hold your breath, grit your teeth, and force yourself to do it. To your great surprise, people will not only give you the praise you want—if you have picked them with discrimination—but they will be pleased and flattered that you have asked it of *them*. Instead of receiving the disapproval and humiliation and scorn you expected, you will not only get the praise you sought but you will gain a closer relationship than the one you had before. The experience will be so positive that it will be easier the second time around, and still easier the third. After you have done it often enough—with the companion anxiety and difficulty—it will become relatively effortless, just as driving a car or riding a bicycle did after practice.

Then you will have opened the door to receiving and taking in the supplies your psyche and your sense of well-being so badly need. Success will breed success, and you will be able to overcome the blocks that have kept you from enjoying your accomplishments, from taking in the praise you deserve from them and being able to love yourself unashamedly. Once this happens, life can be quite different for you. You can stop needing to concentrate so much on your physical or emotional self or *your problems*. You will be much freer to take that energy you had to invest in paying attention to yourself in *the wrong way*—by being self-centered and by worrying about your health or your appearance or your acceptability—and you will be able to pay attention to yourself in *the right way*, by being conscious of what in your environment pleases you or enhances you or gratifies you. That, in my opinion, is what life is really all about—knowing what you need, knowing what is out there to fulfill that need and being free of hang-ups about going out to get it. That sounds pretty simple. But when you realize that your own true love should be, must be, yourself, and that you are not ashamed of that realization, you can go about enhancing your self-esteem and increasing the degree to which you feel good about yourself.

Index

Learn to live with somebody... yourself.

Available at your bookstore or use this coupon.

___ HOW TO BE YOUR OWN BEST FRIEND, Mildred Newman
& Bernard Berkowitz with Jean Owen   28379   1.95
This highly-praised book by practicing psychoanalysts tells you how to
make yourself a little bit happier . . . just enough to make a difference.

___ HOW TO BE AWAKE AND ALIVE, Mildred Newman
& Bernard Berkowitz   25139   1.75
Using the same patient-to-analyst format that made How To Be Your Own
Best Friend so easy to understand, the authors guide you to a deeper un-
derstanding of the past for a happier and more satisfying life.

___ FROM SAD TO GLAD, Nathan Kline, M.D.   28502   2.50
The remarkable treatment that has brought happiness back to thousands
by "the ultimate specialist on depression. . . ."—NEW YORK MAGAZINE

___ GAMES PEOPLE PLAY, Eric Berne, M.D.   28469   2.50
The basic handbook of transactional analysis that explores the roles
people assume and the games they play with each other every day of
their lives.

___ CONTACT: The First Four Minutes, Leonard Zunin
with Natalie Zunin   24697   1.95
Explores the four-minute barrier . . . the short moments when establish-
ing relationships, social, family, business, and sexual, are satisfied or
denied.

___ TRANSACTIONAL ANALYSIS IN PSYCHOTHERAPY,
Eric Berne, M.D.   28474   2.50
This classic handbook describes a unified system of individual and social
psychiatry for dealing with almost every type of mental disturbance.

___ THE CONQUEST OF FRUSTRATION, Maxwell Maltz, M.D.
& Raymond C. Barker, D.D.   27995   2.25
A dynamic program for overcoming frustration, despair and disappoint-
ment by using the principles of science and religion.

BB   **BALLANTINE MAIL SALES**
Dept. LG, 201 E. 50th St., New York, N.Y. 10022

Please send me the BALLANTINE or DEL REY BOOKS I have
checked above. I am enclosing $. . . . . (add 35¢ per copy to
cover postage and handling). Send check or money order — no
cash or C.O.D.'s please. Prices and numbers are subject to change
without notice.

Name_____

Address_____

City_____State_____Zip Code_____
Allow at least 4 weeks for delivery.   G-10